THE
BLACK
PARADOX

BY: JULIUS H. BROWN RN AND GURU ERIC WINFREE

Lulu.com publishing

TABLE OF CONTENTS

To: Raquel, who is my compass in the storm of life.
To: my children who are the destination of my journey.
To: Adie and Alanah the benefactors of change.
  IKAWLANG
To: Jeanne, the one who helped me realize the potential of my being.
  Ami to fu
To: Mom, Thank you for my life.

Our deepest fear is not that we are inadequate.
Our deepest fear is that we are powerful beyond measure.
It is our light, not our darkness, that most frightens us.
Your playing small does not serve the world.
There is nothing enlightened about shrinking so that other people won't feel insecure around you.
We are all meant to shine as children do.
It's not just in some of us; it's in everyone.
And as we let our own lights shine, we unconsciously give other people the permission to do the same.
As we are liberated from our own fear, our presence automatically liberates others.

UNKNOWN AUTHOR

Forward

When my brother and his best friend, asked me to write the forward for this book I was immediately presented with a few challenges. I realized the awesome task of introducing a book and topic of such importance. Secondly, to do the book justice, which it richly deserves. Finally, recognizing the need to be tactful and not say too much, so that the curious peruser would prejudge the work and not dig deep into its core.

So then where to begin? First this work has been a labor of love for the truth. A love of traditional norms and standards at the very same time it finds those forms of historical propaganda, designed to mislead and enslave, wholly repugnant. It is important for every reader to reserve judgment until both authors have been allowed the courtesy of establishing their case. The evidence presented will demand a verdict from each and every reader. Some will differ on the conclusions drawn but the facts do speak for themselves. One only needs to come to read with their integrity in tact and intellectual honesty.

It is refreshing to see sound historical documentation as the basis for this work. It is in many senses a mirror that will transform anyone who looks carefully at the facts presented with objectivity to a freed mind ready to believe and seek the truth. Perhaps one of the most compelling things this book details is the explanation of how we arrived at the place we now reside, and what we must do to regain our footing, if we are ever to advance to our rightful place in society.

It is no mistake that this book is written by two Afro-American men. It is no mistake that this book appears at such a time as this. It is my sincere hope that this book will be fairly evaluated and received in the spirit that it has been offered. The truth often divides, like a two edged sword, slicing truth from lie. In a day when unity is preached and proclaimed; it is again necessary that unity be based on the truth.

Michael Brown
Award Winning Poet and Author

The Black Paradox
By: Julius H. Brown and Eric Winfree

Initial Thoughts:

It is a rare circumstance that you find two individuals that agree on all major issues. This is the situation that Julius and Eric have found themselves in over the past 29 years. Although, there were many differences in their lives there were many more important similarities.

For years growing up as young black men we struggled against the status quo that was holding the black community back. We struggled because we saw things differently than the people that we were surrounded by. Through their 29-year friendship and both being raised with similar values, we were drawn to follow the path of conservatism. Through the years and many successes we came to the following conclusions:

- The Black Community doesn't know the true history of civil rights
- The Black race has been lied to and used by the liberal politicians
- The leadership of the black race have sold out those who they were to serve
- The black church has failed the black community
- The black community has de-prioritized God and has elevated government as their new savior
- The government programs that were thought to help blacks are leading to its destruction.
- Blacks have become their own worse enemy.

We found it necessary to bring the truth to light, for only by knowing the truth and looking it square in the eye do we, as black people, have a chance to prosper in the future. In chapter 1 we tell our individual stories of how our parents raised us with conservative values but claimed liberalism. The first half of the chapter is the story of Julius H. Brown; the second half is the story of Eric M.Winfree.

Chapter 1a: HOW COULD A LIBERAL RAISE A CONSERVATIVE?
(JULIUS)

After reading the title to this first chapter you've probably asked yourself is there truly such a thing as a black conservative? You probably said to yourself if a black man in America is a conservative he's either an Uncle Tom or some sellout who doesn't know where he came from. I beg to differ. I am, and have always been a black conservative, a proud member of the Republican Party and a black man who loves my people. From a very young age I started paying attention to politics and had a good understanding of the different philosophies of the two main political parties.

I was raised by black parents who like 90% of Black America identified themselves with the Democratic Party. My parents raised my five siblings and me, as did most Black Americans, in the Church. Church was a major part of our lives. It was where we found our strength, our guidance, and the one place where a Black American felt love and respect. It was our country club.

We attended an American Baptist Church in the city of Syracuse, New York the name was Bethany Baptist Church. This church was deeply rooted in the history of the civil rights. Our most famous former-member was Harriet Tubman, the well-known escaped slave and conductor of the Underground Railroad. My father was very involved in the events and happenings in Syracuse and was well respected. I remember many conversations he had with people: subjects ranging from the civil rights struggle to educating our people. Usually these conversations took place while we were waiting to go home after a three to four hour church service. The values and morals that we were taught came from the church. So as I started to grow older and became more and more interested in politics I started to notice that the lessons that my parents taught me and the lives that they were living were consistent with the message given by the conservative party, and I came to believe that the vehicle of conservatism was going down the road that led not only to my personal success, but to success for the black race and the whole country.

I was raised in the small suburb of North Syracuse, New York. My family was one of about five black families in the area. Even though we didn't live in an urban area we were taught the lessons of the struggles that many had endured so that we could enjoy the rights we had .We were taught to be proud of our heritage, and we were taught to be the best we could be at what ever we did. My Father, James H. Brown Sr., worked at General Electric as a Supervisor of Human Relations. He started working at GE in the late 1950's. I remember him telling me stories of how he had broken the color barriers in certain jobs at GE, and some of the difficulties that he endured. Through all he told us, he always stressed not to hate an entire race for the actions of some. So I never grew up hating white people. I always judged all people on my personal experiences that I had with them. My father had a saying that Assholes came in every color.

My father always kept a positive can do attitude, and never taught us that all white people were bad. He also taught us to be proud, and if we studied hard in school we would get good grades. He didn't teach us that because we were black that we were some how disabled by nature. We were taught that the only limitations that we had been the ones we created for ourselves, and also that an education was the only thing that no one could ever take away from you.

From my father I received that can do attitude. I never let race be an excuse for any failures that I had. We were taught that if you fail to get up, dust off, and try again. My parents held us accountable for our actions, and my parents held high standards that we were expected to reach. My brothers and I started a joke that my father spanked us once a week for the things that we got away with. There wasn't much that we got away with.

My father was a dedicated father. My mother suffered from mental illness since before I was born. When I was 11 years old my parents divorced after many separations and what I now see as good attempts to try to keep it together for the kids. My father moved to the city and we moved to an apartment. Although my father didn't live with us, he never neglected any of our needs. He stayed involved in our lives, from attending parent teacher meetings to sitting on the sidelines for every Pop Warner football game. I remember my father telling me that "had I not left that I would not have been any good to you." I later came to understand this.

My father was always teaching, explaining why he did things the way he did. He stressed the importance of honesty and integrity. That a man's word is his bond, and that we have to give a good days work, and then we get a good days pay. He taught us to love God, and to follow his commandments, and that there is a higher moral standard than what makes me feel good.

When I was 13 years old my mother was no longer able to raise me. My father seeing that I needed a more disciplined approach to my daily life, filed for sole custody of me. My father has always stepped up to whatever challenges that life presented He never ran away and never made excuses.

As I got older my father and I started to discuss current events and life in general. He expressed strong opposition to the Republican Party. I didn't understand why, but my father felt that the liberals were more interested in helping blacks to advance. 90% of Black American's vote for the Democratic Party, and the Republicans never supported programs like welfare or affirmative action. These were programs that were meant to help blacks out of poverty and to equalize the hunt for the American dream. But I didn't see things that way. I thought that only through hard work and furthering our education could we achieve our dreams of equality. That nothing in life was free; I saw the welfare system as the new form of slavery .If the government was going to give you money why would some people want to get a job? Why would they want to struggle to improve themselves? I saw many people on welfare and it drained them of all pride and ambition, and gave a self-defeating message to their children. I saw affirmative action as a program that said that minorities weren't as capable as their white counterparts and that we needed government intervention to succeed. I couldn't understand why my father supported a political party that believed these things. The message that I got from the conservatives was that if you work hard you would succeed. Let no barrier stop you from reaching your goals. I didn't believe that I was inferior.

At eighteen I joined the United States Marine Corps. I found in the Marines you were judged by your action. I met people from all different parts of the country. I met some that had a positive influence on me and many that had a negative one. One particular person that I met was named Bob W. Bob did the same job as I; we were both laser optic technicians, which was a job that you had to be fairly intelligent to do. After many conversations with Bob he felt the need to reveal his racial prejudice. Bob told me that he felt that white people were just smarter than black people, and had higher morals. Even before Bob had revealed these feelings to me I had never had much respect for him or his opinion. So I told Bob that I felt that it was best if he treated me as a professional and I would treat him the same, and that I was sure that we would get along fine. I think that Bob's biggest surprise was that I didn't blow up at him and call him the racist that he was. As I said, I knew who I was and what my abilities were, and I could care less what an idiot thinks of me. Through the years that I was stationed with Bob we had a very cordial friendship .He always treated me with respect.

From the time I moved to the city and all through high school until present day I was told I didn't act black, because I didn't speak with an urban slang. I was harassed in school and called a white boy because I got good grades. I couldn't be black because I believed that the path of true equality for the black race goes through the self-reliant message of conservatism, and that I am not black because I refused to use my skin color as an excuse for failure. I struggled with my alienation from most of the blacks that I knew until I decided that those people, who had low standards, could not define what a black person should be. The black community is diverse. We all don't think the same, act the same, or vote the same.

The one common factor to Black America has been a strong foundation in the church. Since the days of slavery we have looked to the church for guidance, strength, and even our leadership. So here is the paradox the main reference for the black community has been the church. The beliefs that are held by the Liberals and the Democratic Party are in direct opposition to the life we live through the church .The church has preached against abortion, free love, out of wedlock sex, the gay life style, and the removal of prayer from schools. Liberal politicians have systemically taken away the rights of parents to properly discipline their children thus releasing unruly and undisciplined children onto or society. The Republican Party has held firm to the foundational teaching that this country was founded on. So I ask all of you who fill the pews on any given Sunday. Where is your allegiance?

Chapter 1b:

HOW COULD A LIBERAL RAISE A CONSERVATIVE
(Eric)

I'm what you can call a traditional conservative. I am a firm believer in freedom and the freedom protecting power of our constitution. I believe that governments serve best when they are unnoticed by its people. I have faith in the innovations and inventions of free people, this is why free societies prosper and oppressive societies are stuck somewhere between the 12th and 16th centuries. I also believe all men are equal in every way and share the same instincts. Freedom, security, and happiness are wants of all men. We want to be respected by our peers, admired by our children, and loved by our women. In what country are these things not important? What race of men looks down on these things? The answer is none. We all want to be free, happy, and secure. I've known this all my life. What's great about our country is this level of freedom is obtainable by all of its citizens. Especially minorities, strange to here a black man say that nowadays, but it's true. The facts are there is no better place in the world where the black man has more equality or opportunity than the

United States. My question is why aren't our so-called black leaders telling us this? I know what you're thinking, how did a black man become a conservative? The answer is I was raised this way. Hard to believe but a single black woman is responsible for my conservatism, she just didn't know it.

If you ever watched a daytime talk show you would think that everyone was tormented or traumatized in their childhood .I couldn't identify with this because I loved my childhood. My generation was probably the last generation of real kids. I mean we were free, we had real adventures, give us a bike and you just gave us the world. We didn't need structured activities we made our own. We didn't need midnight basketball we played ball any time we wanted to. I remember riding our bikes from the city to the beach; it took all day but what a great adventure it was. The weekend trips to the roller-skating ring were where we would meet girls, not fight. We were what kids were supposed to be, happy, free, and why not? When I was a kid I didn't have a care in the world. My mother took care of that. I didn't need anything. Of course there were things I wanted I wasn't spoiled by any stretch of the imagination, but I didn't need anything, and happiness is when all your needs are met. When I look back at my childhood I want to hug my mother, because she took her job seriously. She was a real mother loving and firm. My mother believed in discipline, and in my world she was the law. It had to be this way because she was raising my sister and me alone. Unfortunately my father didn't share her convictions, like many black men my father had come into his own. He was living the American dream; he had a good job and was respected by his peers. However raising a family wasn't too important to him, so he fell into a world of partying an infidelity. Fatherhood was more of a weekend hobby for him. My mother did a good job shielding us from this; she didn't want us thinking anything bad about him. Our needs came first even if it meant, struggling with two kids on her own. Despite the lack of positive influence by my father, my mother was able to fill the void of positive male role models with uncles and a strong Grandfather. So even in that I wasn't lacking.

Because of my mother's teachings and guidance we were able to do unsupervised activities such as riding bikes to the beach and late night roller-skating. Destruction wasn't part of my nature, and she knew it. My mother taught me to respect the law and other people's property, and I did.

When my friends and I walked down the street people didn't cross over, they weren't afraid. We didn't intimidate people. Harming people was the furthest thing from our minds. My mother taught me better than that, she taught me respect. If one of the neighborhood parents or teacher complained about my behavior I was in for it. There was a lesson in the discipline. That I would be held accountable for my actions that I must have respect for my elders, and I was responsible for the reputation of my family. My mother's job, as she saw it, was to make me a responsible and productive member of society. My mother never crippled me by allowing me to use my skin color as an excuse for failure. My mother set high standards and we were expected to reach them.

My mother taught us the lessons of the Bible. She told us that God was always watching us, and I believed her. God was always important in our lives going all the way back to my Grandmother, but for my mother religion was a way of life. Later in her life she would become an ordained minister, and teacher of the gospel. As a young boy I was often confused by my mother's politics. They seemed to contradict her religious beliefs. My mother aligned herself with the Democrats and the Socialist Liberals, in my opinion, the biggest enemy to the conservative religious community. Socialist Liberal Democrats support abortion, gay rights, and have sponsored legislation to remove God from every aspect of our daily lives. The Bible doesn't support any of these ideals and neither does my mother. However she does have the opinion that the Democratic Party cares more about black people. Likes most blacks my mother thinks that blacks need protection and handouts from the government. She thinks that programs like Affirmative Action are good attempts by Democrats to equalize black suffering. On the other hand if you ask her does the Bible condone any prejudice, she will tell you no. Ask her if she believes that blacks, whites, and others are equal and she will tell you yes. I once asked her if she felt that blacks were inferior to whites needing lower standards and government handouts to compete with our white counter parts. Her answer was of course not, so what do you think that Affirmative Action is I asked her.

The concept of Affirmative Action is contradictory to everything that I was taught, and everything that the Bible teaches. Unlike most black people my mother doesn't believe that racism is ok even when it's in your favor, she doesn't think that you only follow some of God's commandments, and she doesn't believe that the gay agenda and abortion are good for our society. However by voting for Liberal Democrats she is unintentionally telling us that God comes second to politics.

SUMMARY:

Since the days of slavery the black community has found its strength and guidance in the church. The church has been the very cornerstone for the moral and ethical lifestyle of Black America. After emancipation most blacks found their place in the Conservative Party, the very party that had brought about the end of slavery. Blacks were self sufficient and progressive, and didn't look to the government for assistance. The skills that blacks had acquired during their enslavement, such as, farming, carpentry
housekeepers and blacksmiths were now useful skills that the former slaves could now be paid a wage for. This new- found financial freedom allowed blacks to invest their earnings and start to build their own communities. Jim Crow laws were enacted to stifle this progression. The failure of Reconstruction and these unjust laws led to the civil rights rebellion.

In the late 1960's, after the death of Martin Luther King Jr., the new so called black leaders led the black community away from their conservative God fearing roots, and delivered us into the godless philosophies of the Liberal Party. Many of the white people who stood side by side with blacks in protest during the civil rights struggle were Liberals. The Liberal politicians deceived them also by vote down and filibustered the majority of civil rights legislation .The Liberal Politicians became the new prophets using fear of the past to rally blacks to their beliefs. The reward would be government handouts and reverse discrimination for blacks and a guaranteed black vote for Liberal Politicians.

However, the black community didn't totally accept the liberal ideas or adopt the liberal way of life. Their roots were still well grounded in the church. While they supported the Liberal party at the polls they continued to teach their conservative values to their children.

In order to be a Liberal you must have one thing that is so important to you, that you are willing to turn a blind eye on everything else that you believe. With the Black Community this one thing has been civil rights. The so- called black leaders boasted of false civil rights accomplishments of the Liberal politicians thus leading the flock down the road of the gay rights agenda, pro-abortion, and the Anti-God movement.

Unfortunately this mixed message had an adverse affect on their children.

They chose to take the easy way out into a world of welfare and lower standards; replacing faith in God with false hope for a socialist government. The cornerstone of the black community no longer was the church. The children of the civil rights movement now looked to the philosophies of liberalism to define their immoral lifestyles. God was no longer acceptable.

CHAPTER 2
THE TRUTH OF RECONSTRUCTION

In this day and age, it is hard to believe what is being said about the abilities of Black Americans. According to the Bell Curve study, Blacks can't learn at the rate of their white counter parts. The very language and customs of America are racist, so blacks need their own. Blacks can't understand math or the sciences, so standards must be lowered in order for blacks to compete. The worse part about this trend of black bashing is that some of our own black leaders are doing it. Where did this misconception about black intelligence come from? It's nothing new, these thoughts and policies have been around since Reconstruction. What evidence in history do we have too confirm this? Unfortunately most modern blacks know little about their proud, capable, and honorable ancestors. Men and women who had a nation built on their blood, sweat, and tears, and in the grips of slavery, kept their dignity. The original abolitionist, most notably, Frederick Douglass didn't sit back and wait for a white handout, instead they shook a nation to its core and won their freedom.

In this chapter we will revisit the Reconstruction Era. We will take a closer look at who were the real allies of blacks, and who were the real enemies.

Growing up we learned that the primary goal of the Civil War was to free the slaves. If one was to research President Abraham Lincoln, one would find that he was not the great emancipator that we learned he was. President Lincoln was a protectionist. His primary reason for going to war was to stop the southern states from seceding from the Union. Lincoln had declared that "he meant to save the Union the best that he could, by preserving slavery, by destroying slavery, or by destroying parts and preserving parts."(Britannica) During the 1850's the Republican Party was formed, made up of northern altruist, industrialist, and former members of the Whig Party. They were considered to be the upper echelon of northern society. In their social circles, those on the side of slavery were on the uncivilized side of the debate. The abolitionist found a home inside the Republican Party. Although all Republicans didn't publicly support the end of slavery, the abolitionist found that the majority of the party looked down on the practice (Britannica).

The Radicals in the Republican Party were committed to the emancipation of the slaves, and after the Civil War, the equal treatment and enfranchisement of the freed blacks. In 1861, frustrated by the poor performance of the Union Army, and the lack of progress towards emancipation, the Radicals formed the Committee on the Conduct of the War. Many abolitionists, such as Frederick Douglass, lobbied Congress and the President for the inclusion of black troops in the war campaign. Many of the Union generals stood in opposition. They were of the opinion that, blacks, were unable to learn the strategies of war, and that they would be more of a hindrance than an asset. The Radical Republicans beliefs were in contrast to this. They believed that blacks should have the right to fight for the freedom of their race. The Radicals pressed for the dismissal of General George McClellan, who was a major roadblock to the inclusion of black troops. After his dismissal, black regiments were formed from a massive amount of volunteers who enlisted from the northern states and escaped slavery in the south. Black regiments proved to be crucial to the Union Army's victory in the Civil War. Black troops understood that the loss of the war would mean a return to slavery in the south, and the expansion of slavery in the north and west. Black regiments, such as the 54th, fought valiantly, and volunteered for dangerous missions, and helped secure victory for the Union Armies'.

After the victory of the Union Army over the Confederacy, President Lincoln now turned to the task of rebuilding the south. Federal troops were sent in to occupy key points in the south to disarm the rebel confederate. Many of the Black Regiments that helped secure victory for the Union were now sent to help in the reconstruction effort. President Lincoln was now faced with the challenges of reuniting a nation. Many Southerners, fearful of what was to come with the end of slavery and occupation by Union troops, expressed dissatisfaction with the Reconstruction plan that President Lincoln put forward. President Lincoln, wanting a reunited nation, started taking a lenient approach to a once potent plan to rebuild the southern state governments. President Lincoln took control of the reconstruction policies. He mandated that 10 percent of the 1860 electorate be required to take a Loyalty Oath to the Union. This oath was a promise that no member of the restored government could have ever given aid to the confederacy. Also, only the most prominent members of the Confederacy would be excluded from participation in the restored state governments. At this point, President Lincoln's primary goal was in sight; thus the peripheral goal of emancipation took on a less urgent role, so as not to offend the southern governments or their constiuants. President Lincoln had once stated that it was his desire that all Negroes return to Africa after being freed from slavery (Britannica). This policy of leniency didn't sit well with the members of the Republican Party.

An organized group of Northern Congressmen, known as the Radical Republicans countered Presidents Lincoln's 10 percent plan with the Wade\Davis Bill. This Bill was sponsored by Senator Benjamin F. Wade (Republican–Massachusetts) and Congressman Henry W. Davis (Republican-Maryland). This bill provided for:

- The appointment of provisional military governors.
- Required that every state constitution abolish slavery.
- Each state would be required to repudiate secession.
- Disqualification of former confederates from holding office in the restored governments.
- Mandated a Loyalty Oath to the Union.

Lincoln not wanting to anger the southern state governments, and wanting to keep the support from his party members, pocket vetoed the Wade\Davis Bill. The Radical Republicans angered by Lincoln's lack of commitment towards total emancipation launched a short lived drive to deny President Lincoln's renomination for President of the United States.

The Radical Republicans never existed as a cohesive group.

They were united only by their commitment to emancipation, racial justice, and Afro- American suffrage; on other main issues they were divided. Members of the Radical Republicans included from The House of Representatives Henry Winter Davis, Thaddeus Stevens, and Benjamin Butter. Radicals from the Senate included Charles Summner, Benjamin Wade, and Zachariah Chandler. These men were the pioneers of the Reconstruction Era abolitionist movement. The Radicals were the engines that drove the train towards emancipation and gaining human rights for the freed Afro Americans. The Radicals most important measures were contained in the Reconstruction Acts of 1867 and 1868. This placed the southern states under military government and required Universal Manhood Suffrage (Britannica).

The assassination of President Lincoln led to Vice-President Andrew Johnson's term as President. President Johnson was considered a friend to the Radicals, and was welcomed by them. President Johnson quickly revealed his intentions to pursue President Lincoln's lenient reconstruction policies. The Radicals removed their support of Johnson, and formed The Joint Committee of 15 to ensure Congressional control over Reconstruction (Britannica).

The Radicals passed many more measures for the protection of the Black Americans, over the vetoes of President Johnson. The constant battles waged on between President Johnson and the Radicals. Finally, tired of President Johnson's lack of interest in forwarding the rights of the Black Americans, the Radicals moved to have President Johnson impeached.
President Johnson aligned himself with the remaining Democrats in the Senate, and despite being impeached, was able to remain in office. The Republicans and Democrats clashed on Reconstruction policies, and with no support from the Executive Branch the progress of reconstruction started to be reversed. At the 1868 Democratic Convention President Johnson switched Parties and received a modest amount of votes, but in the end didn't seek the Democratic nomination for President.

During Reconstruction the Radical Republicans were successful in appointing many Black Americans in powerful positions in the southern governments. Among these appointees was Blanche Kelso Bruce, Bruce was the first black person to serve a full term in the United States Senate.

Bruce was born into slavery near Framville, Virginia. Bruce was taught to read and write by his Master's son. He worked as a field hand and a printer's apprentice. At the start of the Civil War Bruce escaped and tried to enlist in the Union Army. After being refused for enlistment, he taught school and briefly attended Oberline College, and worked as a steam boat porter. In 1864 Bruce settled in Hannibal, Missouri and organized the first state school for Black Americans. After the Civil War and during Reconstruction he moved to Mississipi where he entered local politics. Bruce established himself as a prosperous landowner, and soon after was appointed Register of Voters in Tallahatchie County. Bruce held many other offices in Bolivar County, such as, Tax Assessor, Supervisor of Education, Sheriff, and Tax Collector. On a trip to the state capital in 1870, Bruce caught the attention of The Radical Republicans. The Radicals secured many more appointments for Bruce and made him the most recognized black political leader in the state of Mississippi. In February 1874, the Republican led Mississippi legislature elected Bruce to the United States Senate (Franklin 320).

Bruce was sworn into The United States Senate on March 5, 1875. He served on many prominent committees such as, Pensions, Labor, Manufactures, and Education. During the Forty-fifth Congress Bruce served on The Select Committee on the Levee System of the Mississippi River. Bruce was ignored by the Democratic Senator from Mississippi, James Alcorn, but was befriended and supported by many Republican Senators including Roscoe Conkling, who he named his only child after.

Blance Kelso Bruce's term in The United States Senate was marked by his appointment to many prestigious and powerful Senate Committees. On February 14, 1879 Bruce was involved in a debate on the Chinese Exclusion Bill, which he opposed. During this debate Bruce became the first black Senator to preside over a Senate session. In 1880 the Mississippi legislature, which was now under the control of the democrats chose James Z George to succeed Bruce.

Before Bruce's term ended he demanded a War Department investigation on the brutal harassment of a black West Point cadet. At the 1880 Republican Convention in Chicago, Bruce briefly served as presiding officer and received eight votes for Vice President of the United States. Following Bruce's departure from the Senate, Bruce was offered many prestigious positions in the government, and in 1888 he received eleven votes for Vice-President at the convention that nominated Benjamin Harrison for President of the United States.

Bruce was just one of many black politicians the Republican Party appointed to be in control of the destiny of not only the southern blacks, but also their white counterparts.

In Louisiana, Pickney Benton Stewart Pinchback was elevated to the Governor-ship upon the impeachment and removal from office of his predecessor Governor Henry Clay Warmouth, for corruption.

P.B.S. Pinchback was one of ten children born to a Mississippi planter and a former slave, whom the boy's father had freed before his birth. After his father's death in 1848, his family fled to Ohio, Fearing that their white relatives might try to force them back into slavery. During the Civil War P.B.S. Pinchback stormed the Confederate blockade on the Mississippi to reach federally held New Orleans. There he raised a company of black volunteers for the north, called the Corps De' Afrique. When he encountered discrimination in the service he resigned his captain's commission. Returning to New Orleans after the war Pinchback organized the Fourth Ward Republicans Club, and served as a delegate to the convention that established a new constitution for Louisiana. He was elected to the state senate in 1868, and was named temporarily as president of the state senate. As such he became Lieutenant Governor after the death of the incumbent in 1871. At the age of fifty he decided to take up a new profession and entered Straight College in New Orleans to study law.

Disillusioned with the outcome of Reconstruction and the traditional Democratic Party members in the south, he moved to Washington D.C. where he remained active in politics. Former white Confederates that were once in power and ruled with the iron fist of slavery now felt disenfranchised. The southern Democrats felt angered that the slaves that they once ruled were prospering and taking an active part in reforming the southern governments. The newly freed slaves were loyal to the political party that had fought the Civil War and secured their freedom.

Republican candidates, black and white, were winning elections by large voting blocks of freed slaves. Voter drives were held to keep blacks engaged in the political process, so that they had a voice in the changes that were taking place in the south.

President Lincoln and later President Johnson permitted some southern whites to participate in the new southern governments and Reconstruction policies. With the success of the Radical Republicans appointments of many blacks into key government positions, and the exclusion of the southern white male from public life, white males began to feel disenfranchised. They held beliefs that blacks were incapable of handling the responsibilities of freedom, such as, government participation, running successful farms, educating themselves, and raising families. The freed slaves were proving them wrong. For the past two hundred years blacks had to depend on the southern white male for all their needs. The former slave owners had relied on the free labor and knowledge of running farms that slavery had provided them. The white southerners were not prepared for the demands that successful reconstruction had put on them. Freed slaves armed with the knowledge of years of farming began to surpass their white counterparts. The freed slaves, with the support of northern Republicans or, carpetbaggers as they were called, began to build their own communities, create public school systems, build churches, and started rebuilding the families that had been torn apart by years of enslavement. Their white counterparts found it hard to compete with the people that they still believed to be inferior. What seemed like a dream to blacks, who now tasted the sweetness of freedom and the pleasures of success, was an unbearable nightmare to the whites of the new south. With the loss of the Civil War and the insertion of Reconstruction, they had lost everything. Once prosperous plantations lay in ruin, the wealth of the south was depleted. The former slave owners didn't posses the knowledge to run their farms. They were now forced to make deals with former slaves. These southern whites were determined to guide their own destiny and control the blacks. When Reconstruction made this impossible they struck back with fury and rage. It was the idea that their former slaves were now their equals, and the attempt at true Democracy, this is what the southerners rebelled against.

As earlier stated the black voter was loyal to the party that had won their independence. The Republican Party was winning election all over the south. The southern white male of the Democratic Party was now excluded from their once prestigious positions in government. The Democratic Party was in ruins. To the white southern Democrat, removal of the black politicians was essential to their empowerment. To aid in this endeavor these Democrats realized that the power base of the black politician had to be neutralized. This lay in the black masses that were all voting Republican. Democrats sought to disenfranchise blacks of their vote by a variety of means. Some set up polling places far away from the black communities. Those who attempted to reach the polling place found the roads conveniently blocked, or ferries out of repair. These polling place were often changed without warning or notice. Stuffing of ballots was so common that one smug Democrat official had stated "black Republicans may out vote us, but we can out count them." Others established laws, which discriminated against illiterate blacks, or those who had been slaves at one time. Every southern state had its own methods to disenfranchise blacks, and when these tactics did not work, the southern Democrats reverted to violence as a legitimate tactic. General John McEnery of Louisiana stated" we shall carry the next election if we have to ride saddle deep in blood to do it."(Franklin 327)

The Southern Democrats, determined to regain political power by any means necessary, reverted to covert terrorist tactics to keep blacks from the polls, and to harass the Republicans who came to assist the freed slaves. White Democrats and businessmen cloaked themselves in white sheets, and terrorized black communities. Many blacks were awoken at night, dragged from their homes, whipped, and even killed. These tactics were used to scare blacks from the polls, and keep them in their place. These terrorist organizations spread across the south. Their communities protected the members of these organizations. Cloaked in white sheets to conceal their identities, and to play on the superstitious fears of the former slaves, the nightriders used intimidation, force, and even murder to accomplish their goals. These organizations were known by many names, such as, The Knights of the White Camilla, The Constitutional Union Guard, The Pale Faces, The White Brotherhood, and The Council of Safety. The most organized and best known of these organizations was the Ku Klux Klan. This secret organization was started in1866. Its name taken from the Greek Language meaning "secret circle" was started to suppress Radical Reconstruction, and restore white supremacy to the southern white Democrat. They used intimidation, force, violence, and ostracism in society, bribery at the polls, arson, and even murder to accomplish the disenfranchisement of the black voter (Franklin 327). The Klan's First Grand Wizard, or supreme leader, was a confederate general Nathan Bedford Forrest. The Klan reached its peek from 1868-1870. Their membership grew, as their tactics kept blacks away from the polls. In 1871 several black officials in S. Carolina were given fifteen days to resign their elected positions. They were warned that if they failed, then" retributive justice will as surely be used as night follows day" (Franklin 327).

The nightriders burned black churches, and blocked roads with armed guards in order to keep blacks from voting. As blacks were effectively kept from the polls, more and more Democratic candidates were elected to office, and black officials were either forced from office, or replaced with white Democrats, or lost elections that were mired in corruption and voting irregularities. The gains of Radical Reconstruction were starting to be reversed. Federal troops were ineffective in protecting the voting rights of blacks, or in capturing the Klan members. Local governments tried to pass laws in order to protect the rights of blacks, but these laws usually went unenforced by the sheriffs that were Klan members.

President Grant, who was a proponent of Radical Reconstruction, and believed in protecting the rights of blacks, was distracted by corruption in his administration, these distractions kept President Grant from giving the proper attention to Reconstruction. Congress in an effort to suppress the growing threat that the Klan presented, passed a series of laws known as the Force Acts. The Force Acts gave the federal government the authority to enforce penalties on anyone:

- Who interfered with voter registration
- Who interfered with voting
- Who interfered with office holding
- Who interfered with jury service
- Empowered the President to use military Force to make summary arrest

Unfortunately the terrorist tactics of the Klan proved to be effective in scarring blacks away from the polls. As noble as an idea that the Force acts were they proved to be an ineffective tool against the Klan. Southern Democrats gained control of the south and the Ku Klux Klan began to disappear. Its objective, the restoration of white supremacy and the defeat of Reconstruction had been largely achieved during the 1870's. The need for a secret anti-black organization diminished accordingly (Britannica).

By the 1880's the threat of black republicanism had been defeated. The blacks had been eliminated from an active role in the southern governments. Now that the southern farmers didn't fear black rule, they were more concerned with their own plight, and held the dominant white groups responsible for their impending ruin. The black vote would now be important again, but in a different way. The coalition of classes, which had united only to oppose the black vote, began to fall apart. The poor whites of the south came to distrust the traditional Confederate, for many reasons.

An agricultural depression, caused largely by over expansion and increased production, settled down on the south after 1870. The panic of 1873 was especially disastrous because thousands of small farmers lost their land. In their distress they turned on the financiers that took their farms, the railroads that charged excessive rates, but received subsidies from the state and federal governments, the corporations that sought higher tariffs, and charged higher prices for farm equipment, and the democratically controlled government that steadily raised taxes. In the south a significant change in the Democratic Party leadership had taken place. It no longer followed the traditional plantation owner, with whom the small farmer felt he had something in common; industrialist and merchants, who the small farmer hated, started to dominate the party. The radical farmers, who wanted regulation of the railroads, state aid for agriculture, and higher taxes on corporations, did not take to these new leaders, and consequently wavered in their support for them. The threat of the black balance of power did not frighten hungry white farmers, whose lack of concern with race alarmed local Democrats (Franklin 336).

Farmers unions flourished all over the south after the Civil War. They were attracting thousands of farmers by 1870, but they were kept in the boundaries of the south, because of the greater concern of the disenfranchisement of blacks. Frustrated by depression, however, the southern farmers organized and adopted a radical program. By 1889 The Southern Farmers Alliance had branches in every southern state. Although they did not admit black members, they did believe the blacks should be aligned in a similar organization. In 1886, The Colored Farmers National Alliance and Cooperative Union were formed. It grew rapidly; by 1891 it claimed more than one million members. There were local chapters wherever black farmers were sufficiently numbered. After a national organization was perfected in1888, there was a time when the black and white unions were in close cooperation. When the colored farmers unions called for a general strike of the cotton pickers, Colonel Leonidas L. Polk, President of the National Farmers Alliance, opposed it with the argument that blacks were trying to better their conditions at the expense of whites.

A program of radical agrarianism evolved during the last two

decades of the century, black and white farmers drifted closer together, and solidarity was harder to maintain. (Franklin 336) Radical leaders like Tom Watson of Georgia told black and white farmers that they were being deliberately kept apart and fleeced. He called on them to stand together and work for their common good. Along with other leaders, he was at the time, opposed to black disenfranchisement, and looked forward to a coalition of black and white farmers to drive the traditional confederate from power. Then it would be possible to pass progressive laws especially beneficial to the poor. Professor C. Vann Woodward stated, that under the tutelage
Of Radical Agrarian leaders the white masses of the south were learning to regard the black man as a political ally, bound to them by economic ties and a common destiny. "Never before or since have the races in the south come so close together than during the Populist movement"(Franklin 336).

The People's or Populist Party was the political agency of these resurgent farmers. In 1892 the Populist sought to win the black vote in most of the southern states, and in many instances resorted to desperate means to secure the vote of blacks in communities were they had been barred from voting for more than a decade. The Democrats, alarmed to desperation, tried to unite with the Populist, but were unsuccessful. They then turned to the blacks. In some communities blacks were forced to vote for Democrats, by the very people who dared them to attempt such an exercise of the white man's privilege, only a few years before. Blacks were hauled to town in wagons and voted repeatedly. In Augusta, Georgia they were imported from S. Carolina to vote for the Democratic candidates (Franklin 336).

Many blacks stood by the Populist, who they believed supported political, if not social equality. One of the most zealous advocates of Tom Watson in Georgia was a young black preacher named H.S.Doyle who made sixty-three speeches tor Watson despite numerous threats. Democrats resorted to violence. A black Populist in Daton, Georgia was murdered in his home. It is estimated that fifteen were killed in Georgia during the state elections of 1892. Riots broke out in Virginia and N. Carolina. If black rule meant chaos and disorder to Democrats, the mere threat of it was enough for Democrats to resort to violence (Franklin336).

The Reconstruction Era didn't end on any particular date or with any particular event. It ended slowly with the Democratic Party gradually regaining control of the southern government.

The Compromise of 1877 ended up being the mark of the end of Reconstruction. In a disputed Presidential election between Rutherford B. Hayes and Henry Tilden the decision on who would be president was tasked to a supposedly bipartisan committee called the Electoral Commission. (Boller 136) This commission was made up of five Senators, five members of The House of Representatives, and five Supreme Court Justices. They were tasked with deciding which presidential candidate had won the disputed votes from four states and thus the election. When one member of the committee was replaced giving the Republicans the advantage. The vote was 8 to 7 for Rutherford B. Hayes.

Many Democrats especially in the north were outraged by the decision of the Electoral Commission. Democrats passed a resolution, over Republican opposition that Tilden was the duly elected President of the United States. (Boller 136)

In eleven states democrats formed Tilden-Hendricks Minutemen clubs, they armed themselves and shouted "on to Washington and Tilden or Blood".

In order to satisfy the unrest a deal was struck that Hayes would win the Presidency and that he would do the following:

- Pull federal troops out of Louisiana and South Carolina
- Appoint at least one Southerner to his cabinet
- Support federal aid to education
- Support federal aid for internal improvements for the South (Boller 137)

With the compromise of 1877 came the withdrawal of federal troops from the last two northern carpetbagger governments in the south. As Democrats regained power, they passed laws to ensure that the black Americans would be unable to challenge them at the polls, and would be restricted in what they could achieve in improving their social and financial situation, and made it difficult for them to exercise their right to vote. With all these challenges the gains of Reconstruction were gradually lost.

SUMMARY:

Blacks have always had a stigmatism attached to them; they are ignorant, lazy, and criminally inclined. The research here of Reconstruction finds just the opposite, that blacks were ostracized because of their success. Contrary to what we have been taught, the Republican Party played a significant role in the liberation of the black race from slavery, and an even larger role in obtaining the rights that we now enjoy. The Democratic Party during Reconstruction were the former slave owners and confederates, that after emancipation were successful in removing the tremendous gains that were made during that era. The Black politicians that were elected and played a major role in rewriting the constitutions of the southern states, were removed from office as the Democrats we able to regain control of the southern state governments. The Ku Klux Klan was an effective tool of the Democratic Party in the disenfranchisement of the southern black voter. By using terrorist tactics to stop black voters from exercising their newly acquired rights of suffrage, the Democrats were able to remove the influence of the Republican Party, and regain power.

The modern day Democrats have effectively revised history. They have placed the blame of their sins on the Republican Party. Today's Democrats have used the play-book from the past to falsely claim the credit for civil rights. They claim that the creation of the Ku Klux Klan, Jim Crow laws, and disenfranchisement of blacks was all the work of the Republican Party. Like the Democrats of the past who through The Southern Farmers Alliance tried to create a bond with Black Americans to obtain their vote. The Democrats of today have falsely elevated themselves as the champions of civil rights, while labeling the Republican Party the party of rich and racist.

Al Gore, the Democratic candidate for President in the 2000 election stated "if George Bush is elected President of the United States that he would return blacks to the days of slavery. This is one of many outrageous statements that have been made by the Democrats to try to portray the Republican Party as an anti-black organization, when in truth the Democrats history is one of disenfranchisement and terrorism of the black race. The policies that the Democratic Party has supported such as, welfare were programs that were boasted to help the black race, but in truth have moved us closer to our demise. Republicans have always stood firm on the policies of self reliance, demanding blacks to assimilate to the practices that have brought success to so many in this country. The Democratic Party has used the promise of equality through the creation of social programs as a carrot to hold on to the black vote.

We as black people need to decide that we will reach our goal of equality through furthering our education, and like our ancestors of the Reconstruction Era, we will work hard and not wait on a government program to deliver us the equality that we have long pursued.

Chapter 3
The Ghost of Jim Crow

"You don't act black". "You act white". "Oreo" "Uncle Tom". Many blacks have used statements like these to classify the behavior of other blacks. Where did this concept that the totality of the black experience could be captured by the behavior of a few come from? There have always been members of the black race that have viewed positive achievement as non-black behavior. As we became adults, we learned that the only way to succeed would be to throw off these negative labels and the hatred that most blacks felt from the enslavement of our ancestors.

Many Black Americans have unintentionally associated ignorance with the black race. For years Black Americans were told that we didn't posses the ability to learn math and science. These lies were used to prohibit blacks from engaging in the only true path to success in our society. A tactic used on the black race since the days of Jim Crow. These false views have spread from the southern white communities of the past to the urban streets of today's black youth. Among the poor black communities education is of the lowest priorities. Today's public schools are forced to spend equal if not more time and resources on behavioral issues instead of educating the masses. It is acceptable when Black American children score low grades because the ghost of Jim Crow is still present and many believe that they are not capable of better. While many Black American children and their parents clinch to the belief that they are being held back because of their skin color.

To truly confront the problems in Black America, we must be willing to look in the mirror and be honest about the reflection that we see. The truth is that when we find a black child that achieves excellent grades or a black person that speaks with articulation we accuse that person of acting white. Why is it that possessing intelligence is considered white behavior? For years some blacks that have scored low on standardized testing claim that the test were biased because the questions represented the lifestyle of White America. Were did the idea that the poor represents the true black race originate? We have accepted low standards and the inability to reach academic goals as part of a mythical black culture. I suppose that when you look at it in writing you say that's silly. Why would you want to discourage achievement and ridicule the best and brightest of our race? Well, that's how it is. Evidence this with the current political push to make Ebonics part of our accepted language. When you peel the onion back and take an honest look at this issue, what is Ebonics? Ebonics is the inability to properly speak the English language.

The Liberal academia, such as linguist Charles Filmore and the so-called Black Leadership state that we must be all-inclusive and accept how the inner city youth want to express themselves, and use their incorrect speech practices in order to teach them Standard English. What they are truly saying is let these people stay in the hole that they're in, they can't learn anyway. It should be obvious that the inability to properly speak the English language limits the opportunities that an individual will have, and propagates the stereotypical biases that already exist. Our current so-called Black leadership comes to the defense of the poorly educated and proclaims that it is their God given right to remain ignorant. Some members of Black America have taken the most deviant parts of society and tried to claim it as part of our culture, or put on the coat of the victim and stated the man won't let me learn. Where did this self-defeating attitude originate?

We find its roots in the passing of the Jim Crow laws, and it's revitalization in the current welfare system. In this chapter we will discuss the creation and affects of Jim Crow, and the connection to the modern day Welfare system.

During the Reconstruction Era, Black Americans made many advances. The former slaves were building communities of their own, and were elected to high government offices. They were responsible for the creation of public schools. Through policies of self-reliance they were harvesting the fruits of democracy. Armed with the right to build, to think, and to create, advances that rival mid -twentieth century civil rights movements were made. Many Black Americans built towns of their own that were totally self sufficient and in no need of government assistance. One such town was called Allenworth.

Allen Allensworth and William Payne founded Allensworth in 1910. Two extraordinary men for this time period, Allen Allensworth was a retired Lieutenant Colonel and William Payne was a teacher. The soldier and the scholar envisioned a black community that would provide opportunities for blacks. Opportunity was central to the philosophies of both men. They believed that the disappointing status of the black race nearly half a century after emancipation was due to circumstance rather than color. Yet most of the country believed that blacks were intrinsically inferior and therefore incapable of contributing to society. Payne and Allensworth believed that given the opportunity, blacks could live up to their potential, and in the process, destroy that malicious fallacy. They believed their colony would provide that very opportunity. The colony would prove to all Americans that black people were worthy of their rights and responsibilities as citizens.

Allensworth did just that, blacks used their earnings to build homes and start businesses. Blacks became their own judges, doctors, lawyers, and teachers of their communities. Many of the citizens of Allensworth generated five thousand dollars monthly from their businesses. They progressed beyond lower class to upper middle class status. All this was accomplished without any government assistance. Crime was at a minimum among the citizens of Allensworth. Most of the crimes were crimes committed against the citizens of Allensworth by outsiders.

Allensworth and many towns like it flourished in the south and west .The failure of Reconstruction delivered the south back into the hands of the Democratic Party. To ensure the blacks would never again threaten their control, The Democrats began passing laws to segregate and limit the rights that blacks had gained during Reconstruction. These laws were known as Jim Crow Laws. The Jim Crow laws were laws passed after the failure of Reconstruction that imposed racial segregation and setup two unequal societies in the southern states. These laws not only segregated blacks from prosperous society, they also labeled the black community as a deviant entity. The white Southern Democrat began to feel inferior during the years of Reconstruction. Only by segregating and labeling blacks from white society would they be able to perpetuate the lie that blacks were inferior. Interaction was the greatest fear of the Southern Democrat. Jim Crow was introduced to stifle the growth of these communities and to cripple blacks living among the white southern society. As the rights that were gained by Reconstruction were lost, whites in the north and the south became less sympathetic to the civil rights struggle.

The Supreme Court finally paved the way for Jim Crow with several key decisions. The Court held that the Civil Rights Act of 1875 was unconstitutional and ruled that the 14th Amendment did not prohibit individuals and private organizations from discriminating on the basis of race. One of the most important decisions made by the Court was the Supreme Court's decision in *Plessy v Ferguson* (1896). In 1890 Louisiana passed a law that restricted blacks to ride in separate railroad cars than whites. Blacks protested and challenged the law. Homer Plessy, a carpenter who was seven-eighths white was chosen to test the constitutionality of the law. On June 7, 1892, Plessy boarded a train and sat in the car reserved for whites. When he refused to move he was arrested. A local judge ruled against Plessy and in 1896 the Supreme Court upheld the lower courts ruling. It held that separate but equal accommodations did not violate Plessy's rights. Furthermore, that the law didn't stamp the black race with a badge of inferiority (C1). This of coarse was not true.

Most of the studies that have been done on Jim Crow have concentrated on the historical aspects of the laws. In this chapter we will attempt to concentrate more on the sociological affects and how they relate to present day Black America.

To better understand the affects of Jim Crow we must look at several sociological theories and terms. The Jim Crow laws were successful in establishing that being part of the Black-American race was a form of deviance. Deviance is defined as behavior that violates the standards of conduct or expectation of a group or society. In segregating the races it allowed the white southerners to maintain the false sense of biological superiority that had been practiced through the many generations of slavery. This segregation also had adverse effects on many blacks whom because of the fear of violence submitted to the restrictive policies, and only worried about supplying their daily needs. By limiting the day to day interactions of the races and continually practicing oppression, white southerners were successful in labeling the black race as deviants. Most southern states passed laws outlawing inter-racial marriages thus announcing that blacks were so inferior that inter-racial marriage threatened to devalue the superior white race.

The years of these racist laws affected blacks. Many blacks started to accept their lower class citizenship. In order to protect themselves and their families from violence and possible death blacks took on an attitude of non-confrontation. In the words of W. E. B. Du Bois the terror of Jim Crow meant that blacks were forced to behind the veil (S1).

For most southern blacks, to deal with southern whites they learned to accommodate and to appease. Black men were taught from a very early age not to look a white man straight in the eye. To do this meant that you felt that you were his equal. Black men also were taught not to look directly at a white woman. Blacks accepted the role of a second class citizen in order to avoid violence and confrontation. Yet this necessary survival tactic didn't come without a price. Black men felt the shame of bowing and scraping and the inability to protect their women and children. Many blacks not highly educated felt that their only road to success led through the underworld of crime. Because of the unfair policies of the controlling government many blacks found that they had no recourse through the regular legal channels developed mistrust and a hatred of societal law.

The Black community through years of Jim Crow laws, justifiably, came to feel that the great American society held no place for them. Jim Crow was successful in not only separating the races so that through interaction harmony would be attained, but also creating a ghost in the inner being of the black community which kept them from properly assimilating into the society which they lived. Jim Crow banished the masses of blacks to live as second class citizens and thus take on that role.

To explain the behavior of many blacks we must understand sociologist Edward Lament's Labeling Theory of Deviance. It explains that deviance results from labels put down by people with power on others to further their interest. The significant part of this theory is called secondary deviance when the subject of the labeling accepts the identity of a deviant. Many blacks because society told them that they were ignorant, believed that they were ignorant. Many believed that even if they educated themselves that they could never shed the second class citizenship in which they were trapped. During the times of Jim Crow these feelings were for the most part justified, but the ghost of Jim Crow still exist today. Many of today's Black Americans feel that we are damned to second class citizenship just as we were during the Jim Crow Era. This is just not true. The feeling that education still will not lead to true success and acceptance by society is a feeling that is prevalent among the poor class in the modern day black community.

The crimes that were committed on the Black race during the Jim Crow Era has caused a hatred in many blacks that like any negative force in life has caused many black to disengage from the norms of our society. Today's black youth have rejected many of the means to success in this society and look for an alternate route to the gold at the end of the rainbow. The trauma that was inflicted on the black race has had long lasting consequences. We can see the affects of this trauma in many of the behaviors of some modern day blacks.

LANGUAGE:
An important element to success is the ability to properly communicate. Too many Black Americans have refused to learn to speak Standard English. This is the time that we must look in that mirror and be honest about the reflection. The inability of poor urban

blacks to speak English has caused Liberal academia to appease them by giving this affliction a name, Ebonics. By naming this affliction and thus trying to legitimize it by calling it its own distinct language we accept a lower standard and damn those who practice Ebonics to banishment from successful society. While this deviant form of language may be acceptable on America's urban street corners and even encouraged in the popular world of hip-hop. It is not acceptable in the boardrooms, operating rooms and courts were successful people dwell. Still the liberal states that it is racist to expect impoverished underprivileged blacks to master the language that is spoken everyday in this society. Instead of telling the truth that by accepting this deviant form of communication that those who use it are labeling themselves as ignorant and stereotyping themselves into an unacceptable status in our society. Liberals, such as Maxine Waters, represent themselves as the champion of the underprivileged black community trying to gain acceptance for this alternative form of communication, instead of representing the more difficult truth that only through assimilating the basic language will success be found.

Many in the black community are guilty of embracing this ignorant short coming and accepting it as part of our black culture. Many Black Americans believe that if you don't use this deviant form of the English language that you as a black person are trying to imitate white America. You are selling out or not keeping it real. This attitude filled with low self -esteem has been carried on the backs of the black community since the days of slavery and Jim Crow. We as black people have been unable to view ourselves in a positive light, and have accepted the lower standards that have been ascribed to us as a part of who we are.

The Conservative Politicians have been unwilling to accept this inability of urban blacks and have demanded that we all reach the same standard. They have tried to guide the black community to the true path of success, and were called racist for it by the black community and their willing accomplice the Liberal Politician. The Liberal has allowed the black community to wallow in a pool of ignorance, telling them that this deviant language form is just progressive, and that we all should embrace it. Allowing the black community to slip further away from the proven road of success, and the Ghost of Jim Crow has told us that we can do no better.

ATTITUDE:

During the years of the Jim Crow laws blacks had to endure unspeakable humiliations. The stories of these injustices have been passed on through the generations from the mouth of father to son and mother to daughter. In an interview with James H. Brown Sr. a black man who grew up in the south during Jim Crow. James told us how from a young age his father taught him how to interact with white people. "You were not to look a white man in the eye. To do this meant that you thought that you were his equal"said James. With the success of the mid-twentieth century Civil Rights Movement blacks gained rights and the freedom that this country had promised to all of its citizens. Many blacks because of their deep devotion to the church and the love thy neighbor philosophy that they were taught were able to put away the hate that was born of discrimination and unequal justice. These Black Americans have been able to find success in this great land of ours.

Unfortunately the belief that the black race is inferior has not completely diminished with the passing of laws. Many blacks still struggle with blockades of racism being dropped in their path. These lingering acts of racism have caused many blacks to take on the attitude of never again. Never again will we bow and scrap in fear that our families will be terrorized or killed. Never again will we accept an ascribed status of a second class citizen.

It is often said"spare the rod and spoil the child". However we must also remember that if you teach a child with violence the child will learn violence. This is where the Ghost of Jim Crow haunts us today. Violence was the punishment to any black that violated the code of Jim Crow. Not only were the police authorized to enforce these laws, but also any white mob that witnessed any offense would not be punished for their violent actions against the black race. Black men of the time knew this and acted accordingly. The problem is that today's black youth take on the attitude that if you're going to label me a deviant then that is the role I'll play. Young blacks are tired of waiting for handouts that were never able to satisfy more than basic sustenance so they are now going to take what they want. The teachings of the church are just a joke to them. Their hatred is the driving fuel for their anger, and they're going to force you to respect them at gunpoint. The black youth of today have confused fear with respect. They fail to see that playing the deviant role totally justifies the bad black stereo type, and gives society a legitimate reason to put them in cages. In truth it's not the white man they hate, it's their black elders who cowered at the sight of the white man that they hate.

Many black youths have taken on attitudes so aggressive that their very being screams of violence. Aggressive posturing has become the norm for many of our inner city youth. This aggressive posture has aided in the misconceptions of black inferiority. Black on black crime has reached an all time high in our cities, and the black community looks for an answer from the very liberal policies that fostered this lifestyle. Many white citizens live in fear of the current black youth, and many of our black elders lay trapped in violent neighborhoods. They are trapped in daily violence by the ones who they suffered to keep free from oppressive policies.

When Dr. Martin Luther King Jr. led the 1960's Civil Rights Movement I can't imagine that the dream that he had for the black community included gang violence and the violent attitudes of today's inner city youth

FAMILY AND FATHERHOOD:

To make any attempt to understand the current state of the family in the current black community we must go back further than the Jim Crow Era. We must go back to where the black family was broken. During the centuries of slavery the black family was ripped to shreds. This was purposely done. The slave masters set up a system where the black male was devalued in the eyes of the black female and in his own eyes.

The primary role of a husband and a father is a breadwinner and a protector. Yet during our enslavement the black male wasn't able to do either. When marriage was even allowed the black wife was in constant danger of being raped by the slave master, the slave master's relatives, or the slave master's friends. The black male was unable to protect himself let alone his family members. The black male was also set up as a stud sent out to impregnate as many of the slave girl's as the master demanded, thus, creating a disconnection with the role of fatherhood. This disconnected attitude has reared its ugly head in today's black community.

Too many of today's black males find it too easy to spread their seed to many different women in the community continuing the disconnect with the formal family structure. Many black youth being raised without a positive male role model are damned to a life of poverty and slide into a life of immoral behavior. Though much of this behavior has its roots deep seated in the crimes committed on our people in the past, we must stop using the crimes of the past to justify our bad behavior of the present. Black men must stop relying on the system to raise our children in a life of poverty. We must reorder our priorities and take back our role of husband and father. Only by fulfilling this role will our children have any chance at the opportunities that are available.

There are no government programs that can replace the love and guidance that a father and a strong family can offer. The government can not teach young black men to respect women and to love and raise our children. Many of today's black children are being raised deficient the love of a strong united family. This deficiency manifests itself in several destructive behaviors. Leading to disruptive behavior in school, disrespect of others, and finally criminal activity.

The philosophies of liberalism tout the abilities of the single parent, and we don't wish to vilify any parent who is forced to raise children by himself or herself. Because you are able to do a thing doesn't mean that it is the best thing to do. It is clearly beneficial for a child to be raised by a mother and father.

THE WELFARE SYSTEM:

The severe affects of Jim Crow have haunted the black race in our behaviors and our unwillingness to engage the path of success in this society. Though we may face different barriers than other races in this society, we must decide that we will overcome any and all barriers placed in our path. The members of the black community that have found success have been able to put away the hatred of past offenses and engaged the many opportunities that this country has to offer.

A large roadblock to success has been the welfare system. This system that was original set up to aid mid western farmers has infiltrated the cities of this country and enslaved many members of the black community. Like Jim Crow the welfare system fosters certain behaviors that are counterproductive to a successful lifestyle in our society. Just as the black communities were labeled deviants during Jim Crow, today's recipients of welfare benefits are cast into a role of second class citizens. The welfare system like slavery devalues the role of the black male as a husband and father. Women on welfare are unwillingly punished if the father of their children were to live in the home. This is counterproductive to the children who are raised absent the guidance and love of a father who lives with them. Children who grow up under the welfare system are robbed of the education of watching parents getting up every morning going to work. I learned what good work ethic meant from watching my parents get up everyday and go to work to support our family. My siblings and I worked odd jobs from a young age to earn extra spending money. The idea of supporting yourself was ingrained in us. Jobs such as babysitting, shoveling driveways, and mowing the neighbor's lawn were our early experiences in the work force. As we grew older welfare was not an option for us. We clearly understood that one must work if one wanted to eat.

When I moved to the city I became aquatinted with the foreign concept that it was better to live off the welfare system than to earn your own keep. Those children that held this attitude were second and third generation welfare families, trapped in a lifestyle that carried with it the negative stigmatism of the second class citizen.

Today how many of us can honestly say that when we stand in the grocery line at the market, waiting to purchase half the groceries that we would like, but all we can afford. We looking at the customer in front of us, with a basket overflowing, as they pay for their groceries with food stamps; that this doesn't bring about negative thoughts.

Although there are educational opportunities to those in the welfare system, many are unable to overcome the bad habits that were formed growing up under a system that didn't encourage achievement. At the first sign of failure they retreat back to a self defeating system that will give them a fish, but never teach them to fish for themselves.

The Democratic Party has staked its existence on furthering this social agenda. Thinking that as long as the poor stay poor, and they support the programs to aid the poor that they would have a constant pool of loyal voters. What has been the price paid for this philosophy? Black children raised in poverty, receiving a poor education, and growing up with poor habits and poor attitudes.

The welfare system cleverly laid the trap for blacks that felt the sting of discrimination and inequality. It made poor blacks feel that the government that had discriminated against them for so long was trying to make things right for the crimes of the past. When in truth it was trapping them in a system that was not enabling them to further themselves and engage in a positive stature in this society. Many welfare recipients see themselves as getting over on the system. Their basic needs are met and they have to do little to receive these benefits. What they don't see is that they have been sucked into a system that has rendered them helpless, helpless to determine their own destiny. A system that encourages the feeling that we are owed a living and that the government is responsible for our daily needs.

SUMMARY:

We as black citizens of the United States of America must break the final chain of our bondage and prepare ourselves to receive the success that this free market economy has to offer. We must understand that there is no government program that can cure the ills that plague our communities. We must take responsibility for the shortcomings that currently hold our people in a status of second class citizens. When we do this we will release the greatness and the innovation that will bring about success in this great land called the United States of America. Our ancestors through the challenges of slavery and the restrictions of Jim Crow achieved great things like the town of Allensworth. How then with the freedom that their suffering secured us can we disrespect their sacrifice and not take advantage of what lies in front of us. We must exorcise the ghost of Jim Crow and stop using the crimes of the past to justify the situation that we currently find our selves in. The Ghost told us that we were ignorant beyond education, that we couldn't be good fathers and husbands, that we are only worthy of second class citizenship. Out of our mouths we have cast off these tales, but in our actions we live these lies today. Only through a return to strong families and the understanding of a father's sacrifice raising children with the benefit of love and security can we even hope for our race to achieve the greatness that God has preplanned for us.

It is important for the young blacks of today to understand, the greatest weapon that one-can posse is the mind. Fear and intimidation will only keep you ignorant and poor. They must understand the difference between respect and fear. When people respect you, you can achieve greatness, but when people fear you, they will go to great lengths to put you down or lock you away from society at large. It's time to stop hating the world and start living in it.

CHAPTER 4

THE FAILURE OF THE BLACK CHURCH

To read the title to this chapter one might think that we are contradicting ourselves. As we stated earlier in the text the black church is what has held the black community together. You will see later in the chapter, mistakes that we as sinful beings make can not undo or falter the perfect plan of God.

The black race has always shown great faith in the existence of a higher being. Through the years of slavery, the injustice of Jim Crow, and the difficult struggles of the civil rights movement, the black race held our eyes to the skies awaiting our deliverance from our oppression. God's message was always clear, that our place as Christians was not here on Earth, but to reign in Heaven. God's message was a message of salvation. The Apostle Paul, the Apostle to the church, was charged with preaching the Mystery Doctrine. That Jesus Christ died on the cross for the sins of the world, and that through executing the Christian way of life that we are more than conquers.

The Black community has made some critical errors in their execution of the Christian way of life. These errors have caused us to drift away from God's perfect message, and engaged us in a gospel that has taken us off the path.

Since the era of Reconstruction the black community has looked to the church for our leaders, leaders that because of their position in the church were entrusted to lead the political fight for our civil rights. Early leaders such as Pastor H.S. Doyle of Georgia started combining their role of pastor and teacher with that of political advocate.

One might ask what the problem here. The more these pastors became involved in the civil rights movement the more their message turns to what is known as the Social Gospel.
The message turned away from the Mystery Doctrine and the Christian way of life and turned to the social oppression that the black

race was suffering. During the election cycle Sunday's sermon which once taught the Mystery and God's plan for us was replaced with plans for the civil rights movement and the pastor's instruction on how to vote. The social gospel even though it confronted many of the injustices that oppressed the black race was useless when it came to salvation. Even our great civil right's leader Dr. Martin Luther King Jr. erred when he once stated that "unearned suffering is redemptive" thus suggesting that because the black race had suffered so many injustices that this earned our way in to heaven.

The Liberal politicians, realizing the influence that a pastor held, only had to convince him of their good intentions, and their willingness to participate in the fight for civil rights. They now had a spokesman that would lead his flock to the polls on Election Day and deliver the liberals a win. What the Democrats had once accomplished with violence and coercion they now accomplished with promises of a better future. Yet what did they deliver us? They delivered us a welfare system that imprisoned our poor and led us away from the message of the Bible. The message of self-reliance and looking to God to supply all our needs was lost.

The Liberal Politicians introduced the black community to socialism. They used the pain of oppression to further the philosophy that government, instead of God, should be the supplier of our daily needs. This started the slow process of the Liberals removing God from not only the daily life of the black community, but removing God from the lives of all Americans.

Recently an attempt was made to remove the term God from the Pledge of Allegiance; the American Civil Liberties Union or the ACLU supported this attempt. This Liberal organization has supported the false policy of The Separation of Church and State. Where did this belief that the Constitution of the United States set forth a policy of separation of church and state come from.

At the time of the Constitution many people feared one religious denomination oppressing all others. A group of pastors from the Danbury Baptist Association wrote a letter to President Thomas Jefferson expressing their concerns about rumors that one particular denomination was soon to be recognized as the national denomination. On January 1, 1802, President Jefferson responded to the Danbury Baptist in a letter. He calmed their fears by using the now infamous phrase to assure them that the federal government would not establish any single denomination of Christianity as the national denomination (Barton 41):

I contemplate with solemn reverence that act of the whole American people which declared that their legislature should "make no law respecting an establishment of religion, or prohibiting the free exercise thereof," thus building a wall of separation between Church and State.

Many have asked why President Jefferson used this particular statement "separation of church and state" if not to suggest that the Church should have no influence on the affairs of State. President Jefferson was addressing a group of Baptist, a denomination that he was not a member of. In writing to them he sought to establish common ground with his audience. He quoted a prominent Baptist minister named Roger Williams. Roger Williams had stated:

"When they opened a gap in the hedge or wall of separation between the garden of the church and the wilderness of the world, God hath ever broke down the wall itself....
And that there fore if He will eer please to restore His garden peculiarly unto Himself from the world ... "

Roger Williams was suggesting that the wall of separation was to protect the church from the corruption of the world. President Jefferson in quoting Roger Williams was suggesting that the Church would be protected from the Government.

This error has been used by the ACLU and organization like them to remove God from every facet of our lives. The Black Church has unwillingly played an important role in this. By supporting Liberal politicians and Liberal organization they have helped the enemies of the cross push God further and further away from the spirit of America.

The Black Church's leadership, because they thought that the Democrats were so committed to civil rights, have supported them and the liberal organization that they represent. These organizations have shown their appreciation for this support by going on an all out attack on the church. It started with the removal of prayer from the schools, and includes the recent attempt to remove God from the pledge of allegiance. The ACLU and their liberal political accomplices have dedicated their lives to removing God from our laws, our culture, and our society. The Liberals have been extremely harsh on the Christian Church.

When President George W. Bush proposed government funding for religious organization to feed the poor, the Democrats claimed it was unconstitutional, claiming it violates the Separation of Church and State.

The Black Church must realize that the philosophies of liberalism hate what they hold most dear. Liberalism is offended at the thought of God. The Liberal politicians demand that we as a country must be inclusive when it comes to Islam and all other forms of religion, but for Christianity they demand its removal from our public life.

The Black Church has failed to recognize that they lobbied support from their membership for organizations that would see their destruction. We must ask ourselves are we for God or against God? There is no middle ground.

The Black Church in supporting the Democratic Party has also failed to make a stand against social issues that are not doctrinally in agreement with the Bible. The Democratic Party is pro-abortion and pro-gay rights. The Black Church sits silent, in order to maintain political correctness, while the masses are deceived into a life of sin and debauchery. The Black Church sits in silence not agreeing with these issues, yet not speaking out because they selfishly believe that the Democrats are their civil rights champions.

Supporting God and his beliefs comes second to politics. A very good example of this is the current attempts to legalize gay marriage. God clearly forbids homosexual acts in the Bible. In the book of Leviticus (chapter 20:13) God commands Moses to tell the Israelites"*if a man also lie with mankind, as he lieth with a woman, both of them have committed an abomination: they shall surely be put to death; their blood shall be upon them.*" Here in Leviticus the law of God is clearly stated. The Black Church has been silent on this issue. While some Caucasian Pastors, publicly, take a stand for God, other ministers perform gay weddings. They do so breaking the laws of the land, and breaking the law of God. President George W. Bush has attempted to pass a defense of marriage act, clearly stating that a marriage is a union between a man and a woman. This attempt was blocked by a majority vote of Democrats once again thwarting the will of God. I ask where are all the leaders of the black church? Why are they not supporting a President that is attempting to enforce the will of God? They are sitting silent because they have put their own false concerns about civil rights first, before the will of God.

The Black Church has done a great disservice to its membership. To fill the financial needs of the church, black pastors have deceived their congregation by teaching that God expects members to give one tenth of their income to the church. This offering is called tithing. Where does this concept come from? The Bible gives reference to tithing in several places, predominately in the Old Testament. In Numbers (18:23-26) God commands support be set up for the Le'-vite priesthood. This verse states:

> *But the Le'vites shall do service of the tabernacle of the congregation, and they shall bear their iniquity: it shall be a statute forever throughout your generation, that among the children of Israel they have no inheritance.*
> *But the tithes of the children of Israel, which they offer as an heave offering unto the Lord, I have given to the Le'vites to inherit: therefore I have said unto them, Among the children of Israel they shall have no inheritance.*
> *And the Lord spake unto Moses saying,*

> *Thus speak unto the Le'vites, and say unto them, When ye take of the children of Israel the tithes which I have given you from them for your inheritance, then ye shall offer up an heave offering of it for the Lord, even a tenth part of the tithe.*

The Le'vites were members from the tribe of Levi. God had chosen them and set them apart for the special service of the priesthood. They were responsible for the tabernacle and all the rituals that were performed, such as, animal sacrifice for the atonement of sin.

The Le'vite priests are no longer in service. Since the death of Jesus Christ on the cross and his fulfilling the Mosaic Law, we are no longer under the Mosaic Law. Any Pastor claiming to be a member of the Le'vite Priesthood is either dishonest or uneducated concerning the text. Thus no tithes should be collected in their name.

The tithe for the support of the Le'vite priesthood was but one of three tithes that all members of the nation of Israel were required to pay. Different from our form of government the nation of Israel was a theocracy. So weather a citizen of the nation of Israel went to temple or not, they were still required to pay the three tithes. It would be comparable to our modern-day income tax.

The second of the three tithes is represented in the book of Deuteronomy chapter14: 22-24. It states:

> *Thou shalt truly tithe all the increase of thy seed, that the field bringth forth year by year. And thou shalt eat before the Lord thy God, in the place which he shall choose To place his name there, the tithe of thy corn, of thy wine, and of thine oil, and the firstlings of thy herds and of thy flocks; that thou mayest learn to fear the The Lord thy God always.*

This particular tithe was to be used to support a national feast every year for Israel to come together to glorify the Lord our God. Again this tithe was specific to the nation of Israel and has no connection to the modern day church. This tithe should not be collected.

The final tithe was a tithe collected to feed the poor, the fatherless, and the widow. This tithe is represented in Deuteronomy chapter 26:12-13 it states:

When thou hast made an end of tithing all the tithes of thy increase the third year, which is the year of tithing, and hast given it unto the Le'vite, and unto the stranger, to the fatherless, and the widow, that they may eat within thy gates and be fulfilled;

This may be the tithe that the church tries to hang its hat on, yet we could give good argument on weather or not the church is fulfilling its mission to feed the poor. Pastors have misinterpreted these and other verses on tithing in order to beat their congregations over the head and fleece their pockets. What has all the money that is collected on Sundays been used for?

A local Pastor here in Syracuse, New York has done quite well for himself. He lives in a home valued over $ 400,000, and owns not one but two cars valued at over $ 85,000. Yet this pastor every Sunday would embarrass any member who didn't tithe. He would make them feel that they loved God less because they choose not to tithe. This unnamed pastor is not alone. This practice of tithing has been practiced in the majority of black churches for many years. Pastors are lining their pockets and increasing their personal portfolios instead of feeding the hungry and sheltering the homeless. How many college scholarships could be paid for? How many hungry could be fed? The Black Church has surrendered its proper role of charity provider over to the Government in the form of welfare, while our shepherds get rich instead of using the money to help their congregations.

Now I am not an advocate against giving money to the church. We must financially support that which we believe. But understand that there is no blessing in a lie and that is what we have received concerning tithing. The Bible teaches us to trust in God to supply all our needs. I believe that the church needs to do the same.

The last area of the failure of the Black Church that we will cover goes back to the support that the church has given to the Democratic Party and the philosophies of Liberalism. This country, its laws, and its Constitution were founded on Biblical law and principles. Many statements were made by our forefathers supporting this. The Founders of this country understood that God would either bless or curse this nation according to its actions, and they looked to receive a blessing in setting up a nation *Under God with Liberty and Justice for All.*

George Mason, a Virginia delegate at the Constitutional Convention explained:

> *As nations can not be rewarded or punished in the next world they must be in this. By an inevitable chain of causes & effects providence punishes national sins, by national calamities* (Barton 217).

Benjamin Franklin shared the same beliefs and at the Constitutional Convention, he declared:

> *I have lived, Sir, a long time, and the longer I live, the more convincing proofs I see of this truth-that God governs in the affairs of men.... We have been assured, Sir, in the sacred writings, that" except the Lord build the house they labour in vain that build it." I firmly believe this; and I also believe that without his concurring aid we shall succeed in this political building no better, than the builders of Babel:* (Barton 217)

By these statements and many more like them we can see that the forefathers looked to design a government that had the desires of the Creator in mind, in its foundation and in its interpretation. This concept of God consciousness is called Divine Law. Divine Law is how our courts interpreted the Constitution until the early 1960's when we as a nation turned away from God and rejected Divine Law. The following charts show how rejecting Divine Law has affected our society.

I

Birth Rates For Unwed Girls
15-19 Years Of Age

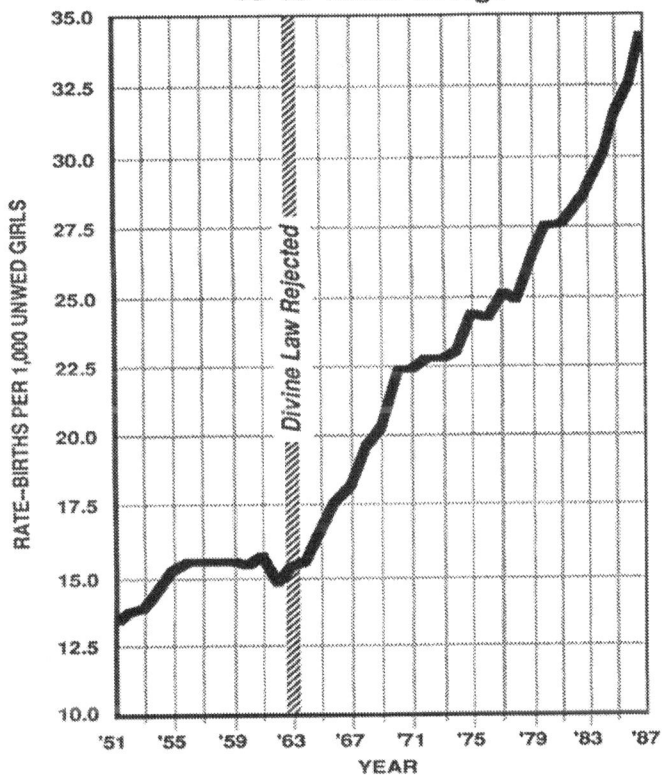

RATE--BIRTHS PER 1,000 UNWED GIRLS

Divine Law Rejected

YEAR

Basic data from Department of Health and Human Services and
Statistical Abstracts of the United States.

Sexually Transmitted Diseases
Gonorrhea: Age Group 15-19

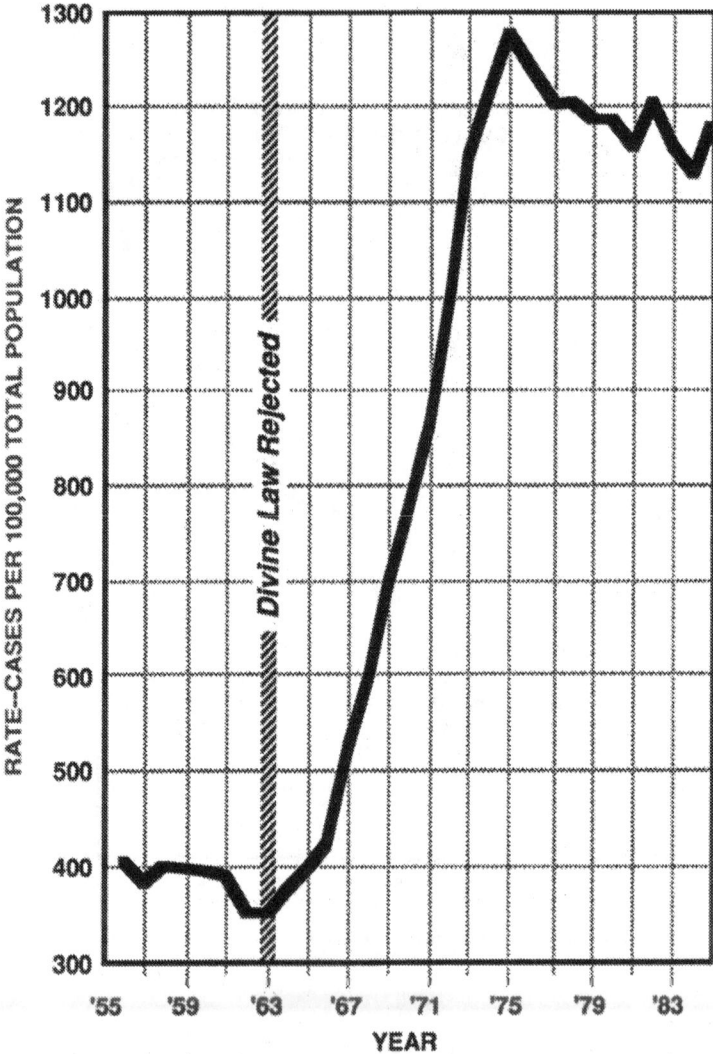

RATE--CASES PER 100,000 TOTAL POPULATION

Divine Law Rejected

YEAR

Basic data from the Center for Disease Control and
Department of Health and Human Resources.

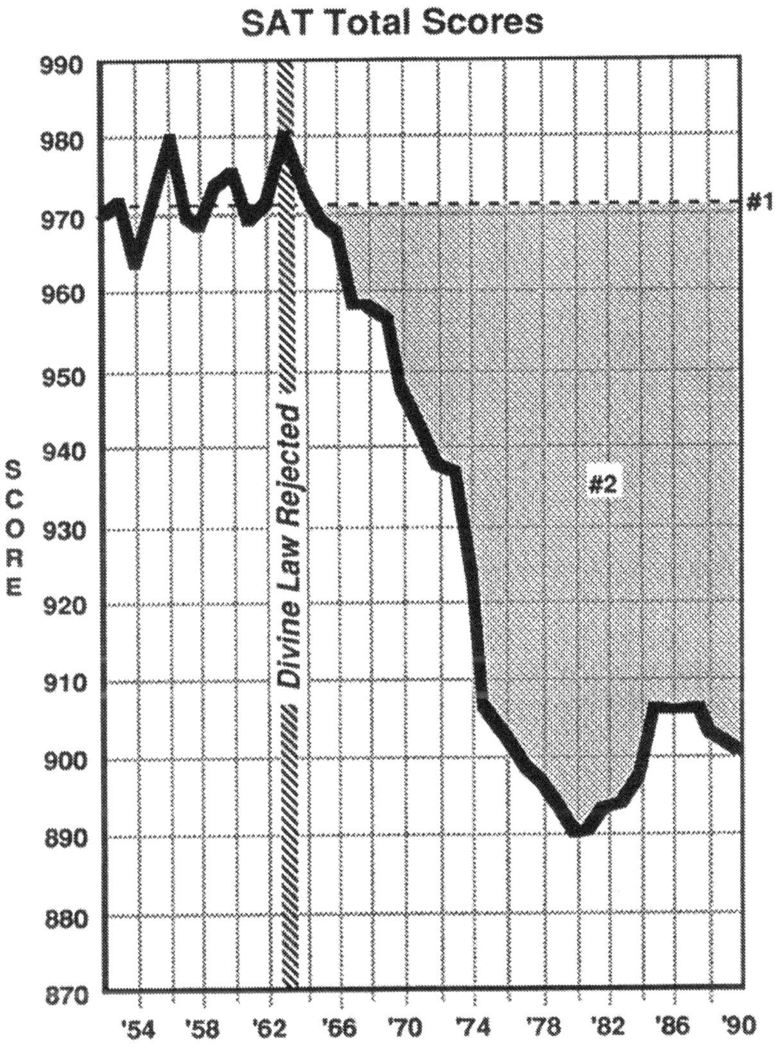

#1 - Average achievement level prior to the rejection
#2 - Amount of reduced academic achievement since the rejection

Basic data from the College Entrance Exam Board.

Pregnancies To Unwed Girls
Under 15 Years of Age

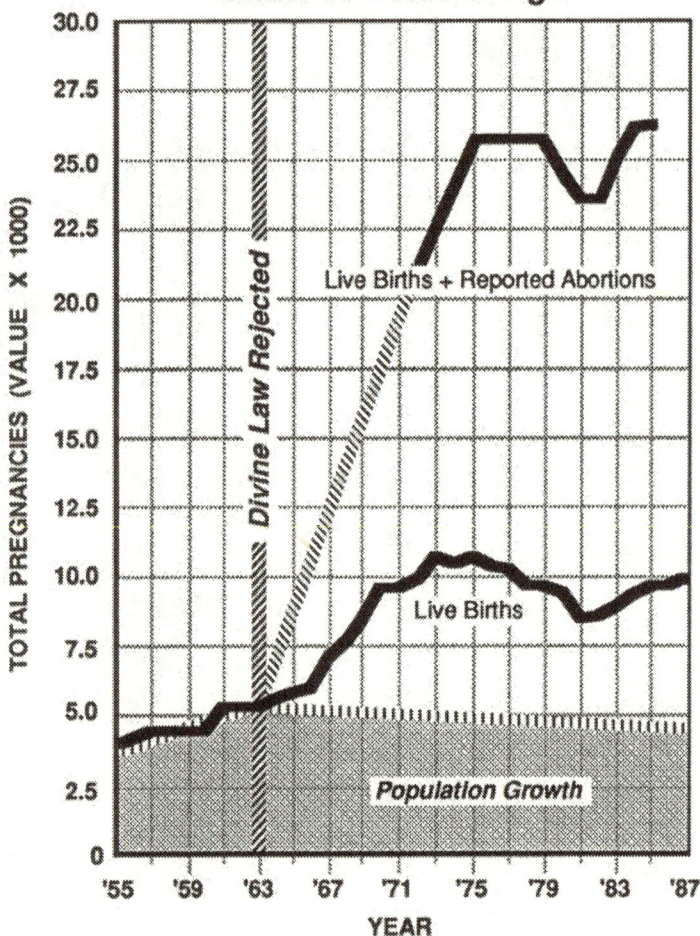

TOTAL PREGNANCIES (VALUE X 1000)

Live Births + Reported Abortions

Divine Law Rejected

Live Births

Population Growth

YEAR

30.0 — 27.5 — 25.0 — 22.5 — 20.0 — 17.5 — 15.0 — 12.5 — 10.0 — 7.5 — 5.0 — 2.5 — 0

'55 '59 '63 '67 '71 '75 '79 '83 '87

ııııııııııııııı Indicates population growth.
ʌʌʌʌʌʌʌʌʌʌʌʌ Indicates interpolated data.

Basic data from Department of Health and Human Services,
Statistical Abstracts of the United States, the Center for Disease Control,
and the Department of Commerce, Census Bureau.

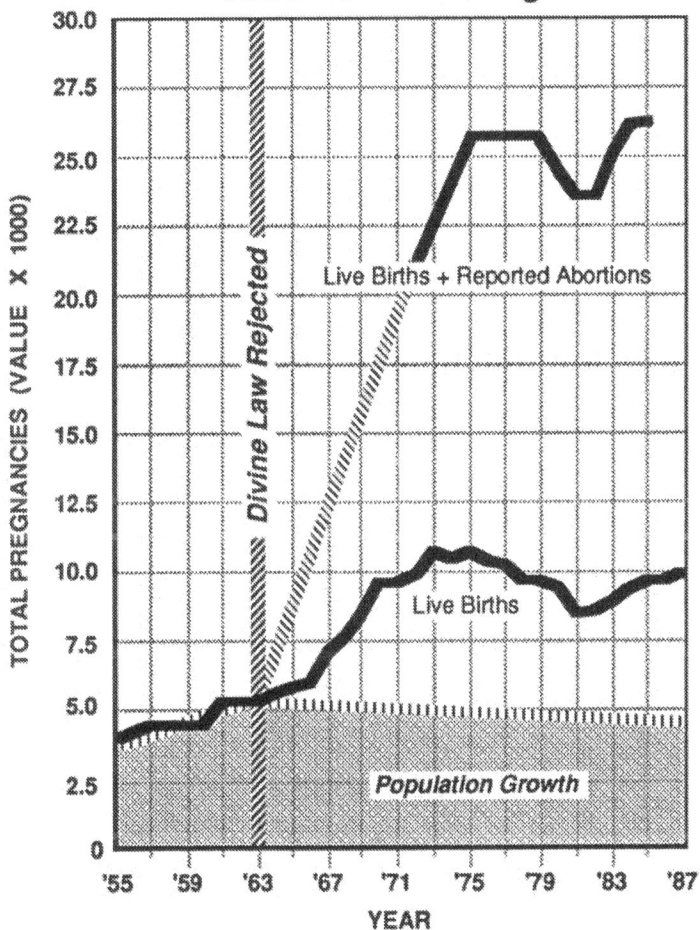

Pregnancies To Unwed Girls
Under 15 Years of Age

Live Births + Reported Abortions

Divine Law Rejected

Live Births

Population Growth

TOTAL PREGNANCIES (VALUE X 1000)

YEAR

ıııııııııııı Indicates population growth.
xxxxxxxxxxxx Indicates interpolated data.

Basic data from Department of Health and Human Services,
Statistical Abstracts of the United States, the Center for Disease Control,
and the Department of Commerce, Census Bureau.

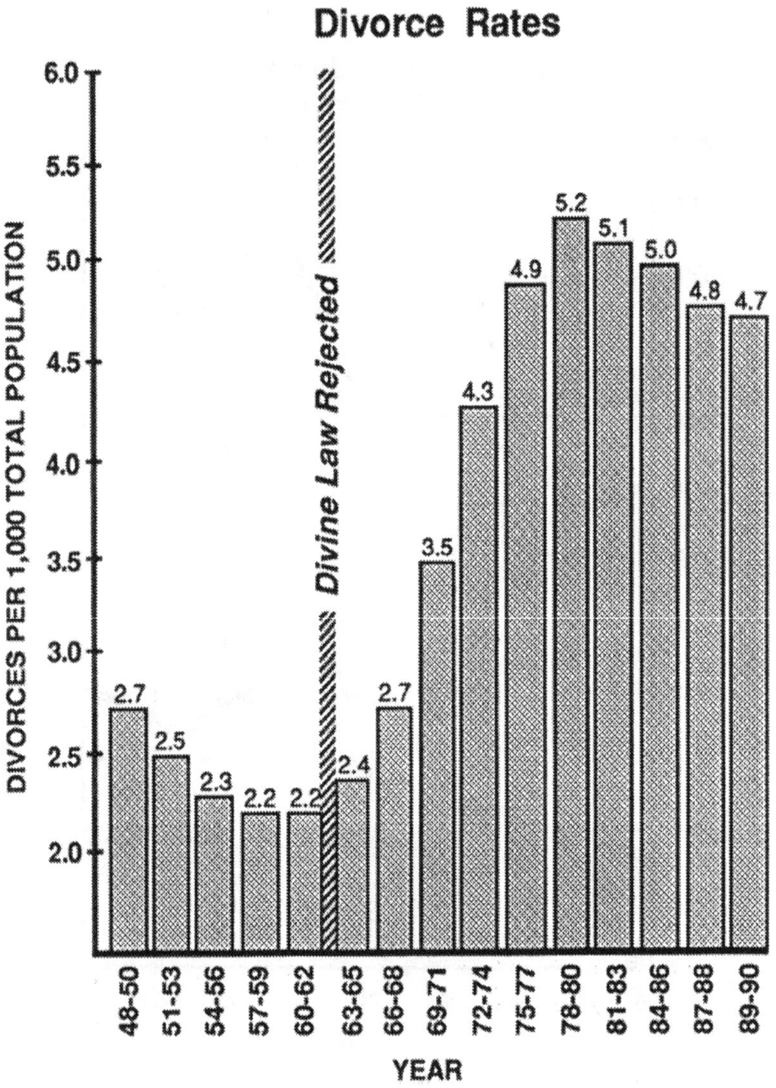

Divorce Rates
DIVORCES PER 1,000 TOTAL POPULATION
6.0
5.5
5.0
4.5
4.0
3.5
3.0
2.5
2.0
Divine Law Rejected
2.7
2.5
2.3
2.2
2.2
2.4
2.7
3.5
4.3
4.9
5.2
5.1
5.0
4.8
4.7
48-50
51-53
54-56
57-59
60-62
63-65
66-68
69-71
72-74
75-77
78-80
81-83
84-86
87-88
89-90
YEAR

As you can see from the charts above, the rejection of Divine Law marked the beginning of a steady decline in the moral values that once guided our society. On issues such as abortion and homosexual marriage the court would use divine guidance to decide. Now these decisions are influenced by the strongest lobby. The use of the Bible as a reference to what is moral has been replaced with a movement that what ever makes me feel good is all right. Our society once understood that" morality can not be defined by the individual." The intent of our founding fathers was clear. The United States was to be a Christian nation, respecting, but not limiting the people's right to worship as they choose. President John Adams our second president, a member of the Continental Congress, and a signer of the Declaration of Independence wrote in his diary dated February 22, 1756:

> *Suppose a nation in some distant region should take the Bible for their only law book, and every member should regulate his conduct by the precepts there exhibited!*
> *Every member would be obliged in conscience, to temperance, frugality, and industry; To justice, kindness, and charity towards his fellow men; and to piety, love, and reverence toward Almighty God…. What a Eutopia, what a Paradise would this region be. (*Federer p5*)*

It is clear to see in this writing and many others from our Founding Fathers what their intent was for this nation. They had great reverence for God and by no means meant to exclude his divine guidance from our decision making. Our Founding Fathers looked to God to bless their endeavors. On June 12, 1775 the Continental Congress put out a call for all citizens to fast and pray, and confess their sins that the Lord God might bless the land.

> *And it is recommended to all Christians of all denominations, to assemble for public worship, and to abstain from servile labour and recreations on said day.* (Federer p139)

The Black Church, instead of holding firm to the beliefs and mandates set forth in the Bible, has buckled to the pressures of a seemingly progressive liberal agenda. We have claimed to be on the side of righteousness, but the voting practices of the black community has supported the political philosophies in direct opposition to what we claim to hold most dear. The Black Church has allowed itself to be used as a tool to indirectly spread a philosophy in direct opposition to God's will, philosophies that have led to not only the black races decay, but the moral decay of the entire country. The Black Church is unable to justify its support of the Liberal philosophies that has removed this country's status as a Christian Nation. We are now left to be judged and governed by those who hate God.

SUMMARY:

The Black Church, through the years, has been the guidance system for the black community. We as black people need to take a serious look at where it has guided us. The church has accepted the philosophies of Liberalism as a package deal. When we examine that package we find that it doesn't contain the substance that we once thought. It contains social programs that have reattached the chains of slavery. It contains policies that when properly executed leave the black race trapped in the immorality and injustice of poverty. It contains a plan that, at best, will make us a little more comfortable in our poverty, but doesn't seek to deliver us from it. Most importantly its philosophies look to remove God as the moral compass of this nation.

The Black Church traded its love of God for lies and promises of support for civil rights. While the Liberals of the 1960's promised the black race deliverance, their majority filibustered the civil rights acts put before them, and the black leadership was too stupid to check to see how their supposed civil rights champions voted. The Black leadership, through the church, continues today to blindly follow the philosophies of liberalism while those philosophies continue to destroy the values and morals of our young and steadily takes away the guidance of God Almighty from the direction of the country we live in.

The Black Church, because of the leadership role that it has been afforded must take the blame for the direction that it has taken us. If a shepherd leads his flock of a cliff, then that shepherd must take responsibility for the death of his flock. The Black Church needs to examine which political philosophy represents the will of God. We claim to love God, but we vote against Him at the rate of 90%. We must stop the association with issues and policies that the Bible clearly calls an abomination i.e. homosexual marriage. We must start supporting the politicians that seek to return God as our moral compass. Understand when the Democrats speak ill of the Religious Right it is you they speak of. The leadership of the black church must decide that they will lead us on the side of God. We can not be fragmented; For God on Sundays and against him on Election Day. Either you are for Him or against Him, what is your vote?

No man can serve two masters: for either he will hate the one, and love the other; or else he will hold to one, and despise the other. Ye can not serve God and mam'mon
(Matthew chapter 5: verse 24)

AMEN.

Chapter 5

MALCOLM & MARTIN

Leadership, Webster Dictionary defines leadership as; one who shows the way, or guides, to go first or to influence others. In order to be an effective leader there are some things that must be accomplished. Sincerity, a leader must be sincere to the people and to the cause, which he has been called. Trustworthy, a leader must be worthy of the trust given him by his followers. Vision, a leader must see a real direction to go, or somewhere to guide his people. Sacrifice, leadership is about sacrifice; a leader can't improve his situation and leave his people behind. A leader can't get rich, while his followers wallow in the depths of poverty. A leader can't eat while his people starve. The true measure of a leader is the condition of his followers, the status of the masses must improve under their leadership or they, as leaders, are ineffective. A standard conservative criterion to measure leadership is that there must be positive results. We shouldn't continue to follow leaders that are incapable of producing positive results.

Over the years, the black community has produced a number of leaders, the two most prominent being, Dr. Martin Luther King Jr. and Malcolm X. What was unique about the visions of these two leaders? What are the similarities and differences of their methods and philosophies? How do these two black leaders differ from today's so called black leaders? What legacy have these two great men left for us to follow?

As we progress through the beginning of the 21st century, we are approaching a time when there will be no one left who walked with these great leaders. It is the responsibility of our generation to study and understand the qualities and reasons that these two leaders accomplished great strides in advancing civil rights.

In this chapter we will take a unique look at both of these historical figures. We will attempt to explain why these two leaders were able to succeed where todays so called black leaders have failed.

Dr Martin Luther King Jr.

"Our cultural patterns are an amalgam of black and white. Our destinies are tied together. There is no separate black path to power and fulfillment that does not have to intersect with white roots. Somewhere along the way, the two must join together; black and white together we shall overcome". (Dr. Martin Luther King Jr.)

Dr. Martin Luther King Jr., a Baptist minister and a social activist who led the civil rights movement from the 1950's until his assignation in 1968. Dr. King came from a comfortable middle-class family steeped in the tradition of the southern black ministry. Both his father and his maternal grandfather were Baptist preachers. His parents were educated, and his father had succeeded his father in-law as pastor of the prestigious Ebenezer Baptist Church in Atlanta, Georgia. Dr. King rose to prominence through the organization of the Southern Christian Leadership Conference. He was also awarded the Nobel Peace Prize in 1964.

The uniqueness of Dr. Martin Luther King Jr. was that he had a vision of a better country. Dr. King was able to see the big picture that the gaining of civil rights was beneficial to the country as a whole. Freedom from oppression is beneficial not only to the oppressed, but to the oppressor also. Dr King knew what course was necessary for the black race to follow in order to overcome the oppression we suffered. Dr. King was a Christian, a true believer and follower of Christ. He took the lessons that he had been taught from the Bible of how Jesus Christ suffered for his people, and understood that it would take that type of devotion and sacrifice to overcome the unjust treatment of the black race.

Dr. King understood that we were not fighting against mankind, but we were up against a legalized system of inequality, hatred, and fear. He understood that if blacks were to mobilize for violent conflict that we as a people would be destroyed. Dr. King believed that the only way to overcome the evils that we faced was with goodness and righteousness. To take up arms would lead to our destruction, however to do nothing and allow the continuation of gross injustice also would destroy the black race.

Dr. King was a humble man, humble enough to learn from historic figures outside of the black race. His belief in non-violent protest was heavily influenced by the success of Mahatma Gandhi, the leader of The Indian Nationalist Movement against British rule, considered to be the father of the non-violent philosophy. Dr. King saw that mere non-violent protest was not sufficient enough to defeat the injustice of the American Government. He understood that those participating in the movement must be of the highest moral character. He demanded a Christ like effort of those who would actively participate in any civil rights action. Dr. King understood that the attacks that would come upon them would not be merely physical, but that the character and behavior of those in the movement, especially its leaders, would be put under the microscope. Any flaw or immoral act would be used to denigrate the purity and righteousness of what was being accomplished. Dr. King understood that the full resources of the United States Government would be brought to bear to derail the civil rights movement. In this, he was correct. It is a well-known fact that the CIA targeted Dr. King and other leaders in the movement. Their phones were tapped and they found themselves under constant surveillance. At many of the civil rights protest local police and National Guardsmen were present, often to intimidate and scare blacks from participating.

Much work went into the planning of any civil rights action. Dr. King had established four basic steps to any non-violent campaign. These steps were:

- Collection of the facts to see whether injustice exist
- Negotiation
- Self Purification
- Direct Action

These steps were vital to the necessity and integrity of any direct action that Dr. King involved himself in. Below is an analysis of why these steps were important, and how our so-called black leaders of today, because of their failure to follow these principles, have dropped the ball.

Collection of the facts to see if injustice exists

This step is vital. This step safeguards the credibility of a leader and an organization. Dr. King understood that to take action where no clear injustice exists would damage the credibility and sincerity of the entire organization. This is where today's so-called black leadership has dropped the ball. Recent claims of injustice defended by our so-called black leadership such as, false rape charges against New York City's assistant District Attorney by Tawana Brawley, and rioting black parents at a football game, have severely damaged the credibility of the black leaders who involved themselves. Events such as these would not have withstood the severe scrutiny of Dr. King. The leaders that involved themselves have had their integrity damaged; thus their effectiveness as leaders is damaged. Some of these so called black leaders were willing to hurl unproven accusations in order to get their names in the paper, not considering the damage that it would do to legitimate claims of racism. They have forgotten that in order to have true justice you must have truth and righteousness on your side.

Negotiation

Dr. King was an effective leader because of his adherence to the first step in a non-violent campaign. He never sacrificed his integrity for results. Thus, Dr. King remained respected and trusted by the black race. This enabled Dr. King to organize direct actions that were used at the negotiation table to gain civil rights. In the famous bus boycott in Birmingham, Alabama, the boycotting of mass transit caused a tremendous economic loss to the city. Dr. King realized that to effectively negotiate one must bring something to the table. He was able to mobilize unity among the black community in Birmingham and showed them what power they had.

Today's so -called black leaders, because of their lack of adherence to the first step of a non- violent campaign have lost credibility with not only the government that they seek to negotiate, but with those who they hope to lead. Many of today's so-called black leaders are more interested in increasing their personal wealth and prestige or seek advancement with in our government instead of truly serving the people.

Self Purification

Self-purification was vital to the success of a non-violent action. Dr. King set up workshops to ensure that those participating in the direct action had the moral character and restraint necessary to ensure success. Questions such as, *"are we able to accept blows without retaliation"*, and *"are you able to endure the ordeal of jail"* were asked repeatedly. Dr. King knew that the local authorities were waiting for the opportunity to present the movement as a violent mob, and this would damage the cause.

Today's so-called black leaders have ignored the self-purification step, among themselves and those who they represent. Today, deviants of the black race are showcased as victims of the system. Drug dealers and gang- bangers are excused of their deviant behavior such as in the Bernard Geotz case on the New York City subway. When a white man was being robbed by four black youths, and defended himself by pulling out a gun and shooting three of his four assailants. Some of our so-called black leaders chose to bring race into this situation and defended the rights of the criminals. This is a blatant case where our so-called black leaders ignored the self-purification step in order to advance their own popularity and attached themselves to criminals, thus destroying their credibility and their effectiveness as leaders.

Direct Action

Direct Action is the 4th basic step in a non-violent campaign. Dr. King was clear on his action, he had real injustices to fight and his reaction was directly tied to a specific injustice. Injustices such as segregation, not being served at restaurants and racist signs being hung by merchants were examples of fights that Dr. King involved himself with. These injustices were clear, with clear remedies that affected people's lives. Dr. King sought equality in the true sense of the word. He sought inclusion into the norms of society. Dr. King never negotiated to have blacks to have an advantage over any race, nor did he state that the black race was unprepared to meet the challenges of equality.

But what about today's leaders, they claim to wage a battle against the spirit of racism. They attempt to pass legislation to change how people feel. They have no clear vision of what they claim to fight against, or what a fair remedy would be. They look at the inability of some blacks to take advantage of the opportunities in front of us and call it racism. Instead of encouraging blacks to reach the standard, they try to create government programs that lower the standard. Some of our black representatives have even attempted to legitimize street slang called Ebonics, and suggest that it be used in our schools in order to teach our inner city children how to properly speak their native language, English.

As we stated in an earlier chapter, it was the absence of divine law that caused a decline in our education system. Today's so-called black leaders in aligning themselves with liberalism have turned their backs on the biblical principles that Dr. King used as the guide and the power of the civil rights movement. Dr. King never would have stood for this. Maybe this is why Dr. King never ran for political office. You can not serve two masters

As I sat waiting for my daughter to have her nails done, an article in Ebony magazine caught my attention. The article was evaluations of how Dr. King would feel about some current issues were he alive today. After reading this article I was left with many questions. How comfortable would Dr. King be with the Democratic Party of today? Today's Democratic Party is made up of a collection of special interest groups that have no real bond between them. You have the homosexual lobby, the abortion rights advocates, the anti-gun crowd, the separation of church and state fanatics, the so called black leadership, the radical fema-nazis, the pro-legalization of marijuana stoners, the radical environmentalist, PETA, and the pro-pornography Larry Flintites. I asked myself would Dr. King be willing to support any of these special interest groups by pull that Democratic lever or forcefully punching that Democratic Chad, all the while having to look the other way, away from the Bible.

How could Dr. King justify an allegiance with a group like the ACLU? A group that has waged war against religion (correction) waged a war against Christianity (Islam is O.K.). The ACLU has advanced the policy of separation of church and state to remove God from all public, and some private, places.

In my opinion Dr. King would not have been able to support a Party that doesn't represent the will of God. The Conservative philosophy is rooted in biblical principles. Dr. King was not a politician; he was a man of the people. Dr. King didn't look to the government to support the black race. He lobbied for the equal right to succeed and for equal rights under the law. I believe that Dr. King would have been in favor of limited government. He looked to have the potential of black Americans recognized and shared with this society. These are Conservative principles.

Examine Dr. King's famous I Have a Dream speech. You find an individual whose dream consisted of inclusion into this society also defined as assimilation. He viewed all people as God's children. Ask yourself, would Dr. King agree with the removal of the Ten Commandments from a courthouse, or would he take up the fight in order to keep them there?

Malcolm X

"God's word is no hustle" (Malcolm X)

Throughout our American history there have been many misconceptions concerning Malcolm X, by people who claim to have supported Malcolm, along with those who opposed his ideas. Neither truly understood the philosophy in which Malcolm dedicated his life to serving. However, I consider Malcolm X to be one of the greatest examples of an American hero that I can think of.

Growing up a young Conservative, Malcolm was to me a great role model. Now, I know many will ask how a radical such as Malcolm X can serve as a role model to one who follows the conservative philosophy. This is precisely what we will attempt to explain in the second half of this chapter. We will also show a comparison between our current so- called black leadership of today and Malcolm X, and show how today's so- called black leaders just don't measure up.

Born Malcolm Little in Omaha, Nebraska, Malcolm was the son of a Baptist minister. His family moved from Nebraska to the highly bigoted Lansing, Michigan area, where periodically he was forced to watch his father being tormented, and finally killed by the Ku Klux Klan. Two years after the death of his father a state agency institutionalized his mother and separated his brothers and sisters into separate foster homes. This is a perfect example of how state agencies at the time had no concern for the unity of black families. With no father or family to seek support from, Malcolm became a small time hood. His eloquence and charm proved to be quite an asset for him on the streets of Lansing. As Malcolm matured he developed quite a reputation, and was nicknamed "Red" because of his light skin and reddish hair. After traveling to many cities, Red settled in Harlem, under the tutelage of a local crime boss. One of Red's many duties was running numbers. A fallout between Malcolm and the crime boss brought about a contract on Malcolm, and after a failed attempt on his life, Malcolm fled back to Michigan.

In 1946 Malcolm went to prison for burglary. In prison, Malcolm was introduced to the Black Muslim faith. Black Muslims or more commonly known as The Nation of Islam actively recruited black prisoners in order to change their lifestyle and prepare them for life outside of prison. Many black prisoners associated themselves with The Nation for protection in prison and as a path to aid in their release from prison, yet Malcolm had a true epiphany.

With Malcolm's conversion, he saw the error of his ways. He took responsibility and vowed against deviant behavior. Malcolm saw these vices, which had enslaved him as tools of the white race that continued to enslave the black race. Many times in his teaching he warned blacks against what he refereed to as the white man's poison. Malcolm preached against drugs, alcohol, stealing, adultery, womanizing, smoking, and gambling. He saw these things as vices that blacks need to avoid because they destroyed moral character.

Upon Malcolm's conversion he dropped his name Little and adopted X. This was a common practice among The Nation of Islam members. They felt that their American surnames were a connection to their enslaved past.

In 1952 Malcolm X was released from prison. Already his reputation as a leader and an articulate speaker had grown so that upon his release he was immediately brought to The Nation's headquarters' to meet Nation of Islam leader Elijah Muhammad. In Malcolm, Elijah Muhammad saw an eloquent, charismatic, and intelligent speaker. Malcolm was put to work immediately. In 1961 Malcolm founded *Muhammad Speaks,* a national distributed newsletter for The Nation of Islam. This newsletter gave the Nation national recognition. With the accelerated growth of the Nation of Islam many in the traditional black Christian church felt threatened as The Nation appeared to be a viable alternative for young angry blacks tired of oppression and not in agreement with Dr. King's non-violent tactics. The emphasis on moral behavior by The Nation yielded positive results and attracted more and more youths, hungry for a decent lifestyle and a message of justice through self-reliance and freedom from the oppression of the United States Government. Malcolm's message of moral purity resonated with those who had grown up outside the traditional family.

Seeing the recruiting success that Malcolm was having, Elijah Muhammad put Malcolm in charge of the sacred Masque #7 in Harlem, New York. This act made Malcolm the second most powerful man in The Nation of Islam, answering only to Elijah Muhammad. With Malcolm as spokesman for The Nation, celebrities such as Heavy Weight Champion Muhammad Ali were converted.

Malcolm's success didn't sit well with all inside The Nation. Other ministers became jealous with his quick rise to power. Even Elijah Mohamed became worried that Malcolm's popularity might endanger his leadership position. After an unpopular statement made by Malcolm concerning the assignation of President John F. Kennedy, Elijah Muhammad used this occasion as an excuse to suspend Malcolm in the hope of curtailing his rise to power.

During Malcolm's suspension, he learned that Elijah Muhammad had fathered several children out of wedlock. This shook Malcolm to his core. Malcolm wasn't a hypocrite, he lived what he believed. He couldn't believe that the man he had respected and dedicated his life to could have such a flawed character.

In 1964, disenchanted with The Nation, Malcolm left The Nation and converted to the Sunni Muslims, a religion similar to The Nation of Islam, yet not under the leadership of Elijah Muhammad. Shortly after, Malcolm made pilgrimage to Mecca where for the first time he prayed and ate next to men of all colors, all in service to Islam. Here Malcolm had a second epiphany, and reaffirmed his commitment to orthodox Islam. Malcolm no longer blamed the white man for all the injustices in the world. Instead he saw that the true problems in the world were that man had turned his back on God. Malcolm saw poverty, drugs and womanizing as destruction in all societies. Malcolm was about to explain this new enlightenment to a small crowd in Harlem when members of The Nation of Islam gunned him down in a jealous rage.

What are the differences between Malcolm X and today's so-called black leaders? Here are a few characteristics that differentiate Malcolm from todays so called black leaders:

Integrity

In the 1997 response to The State of the Union, Congressman J.C. Watts Jr. defined integrity as "doing the right thing, even when no one is watching. Integrity is crucial to leadership. Without it, a leader will struggle motivating people to follow his or her programs. One of Malcolm's most notable qualities was integrity. Malcolm was a man of his word and he was guided by a religious philosophy. Whether you agreed with Malcolm or not everyone knew he believed in what he taught. Malcolm's had no personal ambitions. His role as leader was not for personal gain. His ambitions were for the people he served. Malcolm never took credit for the philosophy that he espoused; those who followed him could sense the sincerity of his heart. This is why when Malcolm spoke people rushed to follow him. He was able to inspire people to believe in a better life. Integrity demands that you do the right thing even when the right thing is hard. Malcolm demonstrated his integrity when he discovered Elijah Muhammad had fathered children out of wedlock he left the organization.

Todays so called black leaders have failed miserably concerning integrity. Their self-righteous, self-serving attitudes are so transparent that their hypocrisy has rendered them unable to inspire black youths to the proper path of success. Left absent of true leadership today's black youths have turned to the street hustlers and rap artist to seek guidance and political ideology. Malcolm warned of this. Today's so-called black leaders have forgotten the age-old principle of leadership by example, and with their indiscretions they have rendered themselves ineffective and unable to lead. In the absence of true leadership we will drink the sand because we think its water. This is where we find ourselves today.

Virtue

Virtue is described as having high moral character. Malcolm didn't just pay lip service to high morals, he lived it. He purged himself of alcohol, drugs, womanizing, and gambling. This purging gave him a pureness of heart and spirit that was evident to his followers. In a good leader there can be no hypocrisy. When leaders fall short of the values they aspire for others they need to understand that they are no longer worthy of leadership.

Yet, today's so called black leaders in aligning themselves to the Democratic Party, fear speaking out for what is right. To gain or maintain power and status they are willing to take the black race down a path that is leading to our destruction. If Malcolm X were alive today would he sit silent as the homosexual agenda takes over our society, or would he be on the side of righteousness and state that according to the word of God this behavior is wrong? Our so- called black leadership has adopted Liberalism as the standard of right and wrong. God can not be mentioned. Without God there is no virtue.

Strength of Conviction

Malcolm was a man of his conviction. His convictions were what defined him. He was willing to face and speak on any issue. One was never left wondering what Malcolm thought. His beliefs were formed by a philosophy thus, even in his absence his followers know what direction to go. Because Malcolm had no political affiliation he never had to sacrifice his conviction in order to fall in line with the party's agenda. Malcolm only concerned himself with teaching the truth. Today's so-called black leaders, especially the ministers, are unwilling to take a stand against issues such as homosexual marriage, partial birth abortion, and stem cell research. They sit silent as our society and our race stray further away from the will of God, and they guide the black race to support the political party that is taking us there. I ask these leaders where is your allegiance; with the Democratic Party or God.

Self Reliance

One of Malcolm's major concerns was to lead the black race to self-reliance. Malcolm preached against any dependency on the government. Malcolm believed in the abilities of the black race to support and guide themselves. Unlike today's so called black leaders that lobby our government for programs that cripple the black race from achieving and define us as second class citizens. For years the black leadership has stated that blacks are disadvantaged so we are not as smart as our white counterparts. They lobby for lower test scores to give blacks a chance at success. Yet, what they have done is given black youths the message that we can not achieve, and that we are not as smart. The black leadership has looked to increase the amount of welfare funding, trapping so many of our people in poverty and stripping our people of hope and dignity. They seek to build government housing trapping blacks in drug infested, gang controlled ghettos. The policies supported by our current black leadership have not worked. They have just left more blacks more dependent on the next government program. This is exactly what Malcolm X preached against

Religious Foundation

Malcolm was a man of God. Malcolm's sought to lead the black race to follow the word of God. Because of this foundation in faith, Malcolm had a clear direction to lead the black race. He followed a philosophy that was thousands of years old. Yet, today's black leadership has turned itself over to a philosophy that is void of God. They claim to follow God in their personal lives, but lead the race towards liberalism, which finds God an offense. In leading the black race towards Democratic leadership, they support the work of organization like the ACLU, which looks to remove God from our lives. Today's black leaders, instead of standing up for God as

Malcolm would have, cower to a political party whose philosophy says if it feels good do it. When you remove God from society justice soon follows.

Summary

It's an interesting fact that Malcolm X and Dr. Martin Luther King Jr. followed two different philosophies, yet had the same moral character. This fact was the similarity that allowed them to be such successful leaders of the black race. Dr. King's method of non-violent protest proved to be the more attractive to the Christian base of the black community. Many believe that non-violent protest was the only path that the civil rights movement could have taken at the time to find success. Dr. King in his Letter from a Birmingham Jail warns the white clergy that his methods were more acceptable than Malcolm's.

"If this philosophy had not emerged, by now many streets of the south, I am convinced, would be flowing with blood. And I am further convinced, that if our white brothers dismiss as "rabble rousers" and "outside agitators" those of us who employ nonviolent direct action, and if they refuse to support our nonviolent efforts, millions of Negroes will, out of frustration and despair, seek solace and security in the black Nationalist ideologies."(King)

Although these two leaders followed different religions they still shared similar values. Values formed by their individual faiths. These values enabled their success. How can we as modern black people learn from these seemingly opposing ideologies? Simple, Dr. King sacrificed with blood and tears, and eventually his life to open the doors of equality. We owe it to him to take advantage of the opportunities that we now have. To do any less would be disrespectful of the sacrifice of all our ancestors that took part in the movement.

What lesson has Malcolm X left us with? Stay virtuous and devoted to God and realize that we have all the tools needed to succeed.

Unfortunately this is not the message that we are receiving from our so –called black leaders their message is one of hatred and despair. They have led us to believe that there is a ceiling on this society that we as blacks can not pass. When blacks outside their party affiliation reach new heights they claim that they are only tokens for the Republican Party
Or they are reassigned to the white race, discounting their personal achievements. Any black leader who thinks we can find success by following a different ideology than the masses is cast out of the black race (i.e. conservatives). We must open our minds and see what other black leaders have to offer.

.

Chapter 6

"THE SO CALLED BLACK LEADERS"

You can say the Civil Rights movement was a Pyrrhic victory. Pyrrhus was a Greek king that twice defeated the Roman Empire, but suffered great losses to his army in the process. A Pyrrhic victory became known as a victory won at too great a cost.

Jim Crow was over and we began to win our civil rights, but it had cost us Dr. Martin Luther King Jr. and Malcolm X. Hard to believe that the loss of just two men could derail an entire race from the course of equality, but this is what happened. It didn't take long for Dr. King's historic I have a dream speech to be forgotten, and for blacks to start self segregating practices, and view assimilation as some kind of sellout. It wasn't long after bullets silenced Malcolm X that blacks forgot about self reliance, and became dependent on government programs and quotas. Yes, the Civil Rights movement was a Pyrrhic victory; it cost us two real leaders and left us with the so called black leaders. We use the term "so called black leaders" because that's what Malcolm X called black politicians that cared more about themselves than their people. In this chapter we will talk about three of the so called black leaders Rev. Jesse Jackson, Rev Al Sharpton, and Julian Bond.

Reverend Jesse Jackson:

Rev. Jesse Jackson was born in Greenville, South Carolina in 1941; he was the son of a seventeen year old high school student. Jesse's father was a middle aged married man with his own family.

Jesse had to grow up seeing the privileged lifestyle of his step siblings; this had to ignite his ambitious nature and endless quest for money and power. Although the young Jackson was quite aware of poverty and illegitimacy, his mother, his grandmother, and his stepfather were always able to attend to his family's needs.

Jesse was a good student and athlete and was the recipient of a football scholarship to the University of Illinois. During his freshman year, the racial tension became unbearable and he transferred to North Carolina A&T at Greensboro where he was introduced to protest as a form of civil disobedience.

While a student at North Carolina A&T, Jesse's natural leadership abilities cast him to the forefront of civil rights protest in the area. He organized sit-ins and marches to protest local restaurant and theater's segregating policies.

In Chicago in 1965 Jesse Jackson was a volunteer for the Coordinating Committee of Community Organization. Through this organization, Jesse organized meetings of local black ministers. Through these meetings he was introduced to Dr. Martin Luther King Jr.

Dr. King recruited the young and ambitious Jackson into the Southern Christians Leadership Council, also known as the SCLC. Here Jackson was fully embraced into the national civil rights movement. Within the SCLC Jackson participated in a number of national civil rights actions. The outward appearance and success of the SCLC was a cover for the internal battles that waged from within. Jesse Jackson grew impatient with his mid-level leadership status within the SCLC, and on a number of occasions had to be chastised by Dr. King for his aggressive, impatient and commanding personality. The truth is that Jackson questioned and was at odds with Dr. King pertaining to the success of nonviolent protest. Jesse also took offense to Dr. King's mentoring of Ralph Abernathy as a possible successor. Jackson saw himself as smarter, more ambitious, and more capable of leading the SCLC in Dr. King's absence. Dr. King wasn't impressed with Jackson's misguided ambition; he was interested in mentoring a replacement who would continue the movement in the direction he had started. Did Dr. King see Jesse Jackson's ambition as a personal flaw to leadership? Was he concerned that under Jackson's leadership the movement would take a different direction?

On that fateful day, the SCLC held a meeting among its leadership. Midlevel leaders, like Jesse Jackson, were told to remain downstairs, and ordered not to speak to the press. Why was it that shortly after Dr. King's assassination Jesse Jackson was giving interviews, wearing a shirt supposedly stained with Dr. King's blood? Since this event there has been many questions as to the accuracy of Jesse Jackson's claims that he was holding Dr. King in his arm's, heard his last words, and stained his shirt with Dr. King's blood. What possible motive would Jesse Jackson have to lie about such a historic and tragic occasion?

Reference this photograph of Ralph Abernathy and other SCLC leaders in attendance at the meeting on the day of Dr. King's assassination. We are unable to see Jesse Jackson anywhere near Dr. King. Reports from SCLC leaders state that he was in the parking lot as ordered. Could his claims have been a power play to control of the SCLC?

Shortly after Dr. King's assassination Jesse Jackson offended many of the SCLC leaders with his public antics. His internal feuds with Ralph Abernathy, Dr. King's successor, and his many publicity stunts led to his resignation in 1971.

Jesse Jackson then formed his own organization called OPERATION PUSH. The main goals of this organization were to pursue economic objectives and to expand into areas of social and political development for blacks in the Chicago area and across the nation. His economic boycotts were criticized by some business owners as extortive and by some reformers as lacking follow through. The management of PUSH'S personnel and finances were the subject of close scrutiny, and the freewheeling nature of the organization was regularly called into question. (Henderson 3)

Free from the moral scrutiny of the SCLC, Jackson's organization operated outside the boundaries set up by Dr. King. Because of his theatrics and charisma, Jesse Jackson soon became recognized as the national spokesperson for the black race. White politicians, not wanting to be labeled racist, felt they had no choice, but to deal with him. The real question is what did he do with this power and influence? This is where we will turn our focus. Dr. King was killed in 1968, it's now 2006. We, as a race, have spent almost forty years under the reign of Jesse Jackson. How has the black race progressed under Jackson's leadership?

Among ethnic groups, blacks score lowest on standardized testing in reading and math, blacks have the highest high school dropout rate, and the lowest scores on college entrance exams. Out of wedlock teenaged pregnancies are at epidemic levels within the black community. Prison incarceration and black on black crime are at an all time high. I know what many of you are saying; you can't blame all of these troubles on Jesse Jackson, that's just evidence of racism. I beg to differ.

Jesse Jackson is the self-proclaimed leader of the black race and all of this happened on his watch, and we hold him responsible. Jesse Jackson has been on the wrong side of history for the last four decades. The direction he chose to lead the black race, the path of the victim, has played a major role in the difficulties experienced by the black race. Jesse Jackson has incorporated a racial element into all dealings with the government and in society even when no racial prejudices were present. On the September 3rd 2005 broadcast of the Today Show the Reverend Jesse Jackson, in reference to hurricane Katrina survivors, compared the shelter of the Houston Astrodome to a slave ship. Again trying to interject a racial element where one doesn't belong. Here he tried to represent the federal government as racist because it sheltered the multitude of homeless from New Orleans. Yet, this has been the strategy implemented by Jackson throughout his reign as a so called black leader. He has chose to carry the Liberal politician's banner and to secure for them the black vote, by any means necessary. He has done this to secure his stature within the Democratic Party. Could this be the misguided ambition that Dr. King saw the seedlings of? His stands on current issue are just typical liberal talking points.

Take his stand on something as simple as vouchers. Educational Vouchers is a conservative policy to give parents an alternative to bad public schools, the program would allow parents to keep a portion of their tax dollars to help pay for the private school of their choice. Jesse Jackson opposes vouchers, he stated "vouchers will destroy the public school system and undo all our hard work of integration ". Jackson couldn't be more wrong; in reality private schools do a much better job of integration than public schools. A recent study by researchers, Jay P. Green and Nicole Mellow of the University of Texas, on students in private and public school cafeterias. Found that black and white children sat together more frequently in private schools. Black and white children in private schools have more in common with each other than black and white children in public schools. The overwhelming majority of students in private schools come from loving hard working two parent families that put education as a priority. Most of the parents of private school students are themselves educated. Jesse Jackson must know all the facts about private schools, he sent his children to private schools.

Where does Jesse Jackson stand on the issue of taxes? Just like every other economically challenged Democrat, Jesse Jackson hates the idea of people keeping their money. Tax cuts are for the rich is the typical mantra, however the truth is tax cuts help everyone who pay taxes. The real reason Jesse Jackson hates tax cuts is his various organizations like the Rainbow Coalition and PUSH rely heavily on tax dollars. Jackson's organizations bring in around $17 million a year, Jackson himself makes over half a million dollars in income. Jackson was given $450,000 by the Democratic Party for the Get out the vote effort. The facts are tax cuts take money out of Jackson's pocket. I challenge you; can any of you tell me what does the Rainbow Coalition or Operation Push do with all those tax dollars? That's our money, money that rich democrats like Jackson say we don't need, the nerve.

Where does Jackson stand on medical savings accounts? He's one of the critics claiming, Medicaid and Medicare can't adequately handle the needs of the poor and the elderly. His solution, spends more money, but keeps those dollars in the same bureaucratic poverty insuring government program. Medical savings accounts would allow people to set aside a certain amount of money for medical cost each year. The market could then force medical facilities to compete for business, and if you have a number of healthy years all the monies accumulated are yours and no government agency could touch it. This is just the kind of program black's need, a way to help us save money. My question is why doesn't Jackson support this? Could the answer be that Jesse Jackson needs poor black people? If blacks were self reliant why would they need Jesse Jackson?

Jesse Jackson has broken one of the cardinal rules of leadership, sacrifice. We must remember Moses never made it to the promise land, his fight was for his people, but Jackson has gotten rich off the pain of his people. Worse he led generations of people down the road of government dependence, and justification. Many blacks no longer believe their destiny is in their own hands, the only thing they believe they can get; they must get from the government. Gone is black self-reliance, gone is black pride, gone is righteousness and most importantly gone is spirituality. Black people open your eyes and stop getting sold out by false prophets like Jackson.

The Reverend Jesse Jackson has positioned himself as the national spokesman for the black race. In truth what has he accomplished? Like many other politicians he has increased his personal wealth at the expense of those he was to lead out of poverty. Unlike Dr. Martin Luther King Jr. and Malcolm X, Reverend Jackson led his people off the path of righteousness, and has accepted the doctrine of Liberalism as the truth and our salvation, or has he? The major problem with this plan is that liberalism is in direct conflict with the word of God. While Reverend Jackson assumed the title of reverend and publicly proclaims to be a shepherd for the Almighty, he has put the agenda of the Democratic Party before the welfare of the flock. He has sold us out to the highest bidder.

Not unlike the past, the slave master looked for one among us who was willing to do the master's will, even at the expense of all the others. For this betrayal the "House Nigga" was well compensated. The Reverend Jackson has sought to rise in stature within the Democratic Party by promising to year after year deliver the black vote. Not unlike other politicians this strategy has brought him great personal wealth, but what has it done for the black race. It has done exactly what it was designed to do. It has left the majority of us waiting in line for that great government handout.

While Conservative leaders have tried to deliver the same message that Dr. King and Malcolm X preached to us; that our only chance to succeed was through self –reliance and faith in God. The Reverend Jackson has carried the marching orders of our former masters that Conservatives are racist, and don't look to right the wrongs of the past. Under Reverend Jackson's leadership we have spent almost 40 years looking to the past instead of preparing for the future. Yet, Reverend Jackson is okay. Like other Democratic leaders he is able to convince the poor that "he can feel their pain". When in truth Reverend Jackson has never felt the sting of poverty. Please understand my last statement; I don't hold it against him that he has never been poor. I wish that all Americans could be ignorant to the pains of poverty. Instead of leading the black race towards prosperity, Reverend Jackson has led us right where the true racist wanted us to be. Had he kept us on the path that Dr. King started us on there may have been no need for his services. It seems that Reverend Jackson's actions have always been self serving and insurance to maintain the status quo. So with every incidence of seemingly wrong doing he was always there to speak for the black race.

The black race has never been results orientated. If we had been would we have afforded the Reverend Jackson the power he has? Not unlike other wolves in sheep clothing, he appears to desire effective gains for the black race. He seeks from the oppressor a slice of the pie. He has spent the last 40 years delivering to us the scrapes that the master was willing to let fall off his dinner table. Instead of leading us to the place where we understand that we need to bake our own pie.

Had we been result orientated would we be satisfied with what has been delivered? The Reverend Jackson isn't, he is always stating that there have been no improvements since the 1960's. This is when he took the reigns, this is under his watch, and this is the road he has decided to take us on. With his own lips he testifies of his incompetence. What he hasn't said is the truth, that he has been an ineffective leader and an obstruction to the progression of the black race.

For those of us that chose to stay on the path that Dr. King and Malcolm X started, America is a better place. Because we have recognized that education is the great equalizer and that success is not a government program. Hard work and sacrifice are still important ingredients to a better life. Blacks that succeed today are not waiting for the government to deliver us success and equality, like our ancestors during the civil war, we are claiming it.

Those who follow the Reverend Jackson will remain waiting on the promises of a liberal government that is unable to deliver what they seek, and the Reverend Jackson will be at the head of that line getting our piece and continuing to deliver crumbs.

Reverend Al Sharpton:

In the troubling times that we live, the role of our leaders must be to lead the masses to a better place. Dr. Martin Luther King Jr. is loved and respected, many years after his death, because he affected positive change in the life of every black American. When we view the career of the Reverend Al Sharpton we are left wanting. One must ask what positive change has the Reverend Sharpton led the charge for? How have the lives of black Americans improved because of his leadership?

The answers to these questions are not favorable to the Reverend. The battles that he chose to wage correspond with the role of the victim that was adopted after the deaths of our leaders of the civil rights movement. Like other black leaders the Reverend Sharpton has ignored the parameters set up by Dr. Martin King Jr. pertaining to what qualification are necessary for civil rights organizations to get involved.

The Reverend Alfred Charles Sharpton Jr. was born October 3, 1954 in Brooklyn New York. Different from the Reverend Jesse Jackson, the Reverend Sharpton was ordained and licensed as a minister in 1963. The Reverend Sharpton was billed as the "Wonder Boy Preacher" at the 1964 Worlds Fair, where he preached impressive sermons and marveled the crowds with his knowledge of the scriptures at his young age. As The Rev. Sharpton's interest with preaching grew he started to tour with the famous gospel singer Mahalia Jackson and others.

The Rev. Sharpton's first attempt at protest was in high school, where the minister led protests against the cafeteria's food and the dress code. In 1969 he was appointed youth director by Jesse Jackson of Operation Breadbasket, a group that focused on the promotion of new and better jobs for African Americans through negotiations and community wide boycotts.

In the 1970's, Sharpton dropped out of college to be a tour manager for the singer James Brown. Here he met his future wife, Kathy Jordan, a backup singer for James Brown.

The early years of the Reverend Sharpton seemed to prep him for his future as a civil rights leader. He, like leaders before him were based in the church. The Reverend, different from his predecessors, had a background in the entertainment field which trained him how to speak and entertain crowds. The Reverend was able to combine his entertainment background with his religious background, and was able to appeal too many within the black community.

The Rev. Sharpton has been able to attract thousands of followers with his brash in your face attitude and his charisma, but what has he done with this power?

When the Reverend was four, according to the legend, he began to preach. Jesse Jackson, who became his mentor, has described him as a child prodigy. When he was about fourteen, Sharpton hooked up with one of the many Jackson's operations, and at sixteen started the first of his own: The National Youth Movement. He was also drawn to Adam Clayton Powell, the colorful and crooked congressman from Harlem. Shortly before he died, in 1972, he had some final words for young Sharpton (in The Rev's telling): "These yellow Uncle Toms are taking over the blacks in New York. Powell stated "don't you stop fighting". If you want to do something for Adam, get rid of these Uncle Toms."(Nordlinger 2)

Later, Sharpton came under the wing of James Brown, the soul singer, who acted as a father to him. Sharpton stated "James Brown was my father; and Jesse Jackson was my teacher". When he at last took to full time rabble rousing, he did so with ferocity, lashing out at "faggots" "cocktail sipping negroes," and even the black Marxist- those who carried "that German cracker's book under their arms." (Nordlinger 2)

The Rev. Sharpton received his views and tactics on civil rights from being mentored by Jesse Jackson. These lessons were learned well. The Rev Sharpton has sought out situations where blacks are the victim and has brought to light the injustice that exists. One might ask what the problem with this is. The problem arises when you operate on the premise that the ends justify the means, which seems to have been a major influencing theory of the Rev. Sharpton. The Reverend has used any situation for his personal gain. He has used poor judgment when it came to the truth of different incidents. He has viewed what could be gained for the black race as more important than the truth, not realizing that he risked his and the movements credibility.

His first major leap into the national spot light was with the Bernard Goetz incident where a white man shot four black youths on a New York subway that tried to rob him. On this occasion the Rev. Sharpton sided with the criminals and called for Bernard Goetz's head. Once again our black leaders ignored the teachings of past civil rights leaders and involved themselves in an incident where civil rights where not the issue. In siding with the criminal many viewed the black leadership as biased. Even in the face of clear wrong doing of these four black youths our black leaders felt it was more important to scream racism were none existed.

This has been a pattern with the Reverend, two years later the famous Howard Beach incident occurred: a young black man, Michael Griffith, was chased to his death by a white mob while this incident clearly involved racism the Rev. Sharpton used this situation to launch himself to national prominence. The Reverend started operating as the spokesman for the victim. He would call victims or their families-or defendants and theirs- to offer his services, which included cash, legal counsel, and the like. Sharpton himself would serve as an "adviser and spokesman." He quickly earned the sobriquet "Reverend 911" responding to any black-white emergency. (Nordlinger 2)

The Reverend Sharpton became known as the ambulance chaser of the civil rights movement. The problem with this was that like the traditional ambulance chaser the majority of the incidents that the Reverend involved himself were either hoaxes, or situations where civil rights were truly not the issue. This has damaged the creditability of not only the Reverend Sharpton, but the civil rights movement as a whole. The best known incident in which the Reverend Sharpton involved himself was the Tawana Brawley hoax. In 1987 a girl named Tawana Brawley, after staying away from home for several days, smeared herself with dog feces, scrawled racial epithets on her body, and hopped into a garbage bag. Then she falsely claimed that six white men, including a police officer, had raped and tormented her. All of American was horrified. Actor and comedian Bill Cosby offered a large monetary reward for information leading to the arrest of the guilty parties. The Reverend Al Sharpton activated, and acted as the Brawley's family advisor. He urged the family not to cooperate with the authorities, including the State Attorney General Robert Abrams. Al Sharpton stated "to cooperate with Abrams would be like sitting down with Hitler." A Sharpton sidekick, Alton Maddox, added, "Robert Abrams, you are no longer going to masturbate looking at Tawana Brawley's picture (Nordlinger 1).

The Reverend Sharpton and his team used loud brash behavior and wild allegations to further their causes. Like the Tawana Brawley case, which was proved to have never happened, the Reverend Sharpton has used the press and the aurora of racial tension to further his national visibility. When Sharpton and two others in his organization suggested that the then Governor of New York State, Mario Cuomo had ties to organized crime, several members of Sharpton's Advisory Congregation that supported Brawley backed out and claimed that Sharpton knew the incident was a hoax from the very beginning.

The Reverend Al Sharpton has made a career of defending blacks, not on the basis of innocence, but because the color of their skin. Like many blacks the Reverend seems to believe that because of the years of injustice on the black race that we should turn a blind eye on crime committed by blacks. The Reverend Sharpton has frequently chosen the side of the criminal such as in the Tawana Brawley, Bernard Goetz, Central Park Jogger, and Crown Heights cases which has damaged his creditability and rendered him ineffective as a leader. Although all the incidents that Al Sharpton has inserted himself in are not hoaxes or in the defense of criminals (i.e. 1997 Abner Louima, Brooklyn N.Y. and the 1999 Amadou Diablo Bronx police slaying of a West African immigrant) his involvement suggests an aurora of hypocrisy.

Another important component to leadership is integrity. In our world today it seems that integrity is too much to ask for, but because these black leaders are taking on civil rights it is imperative that they be above reproach. How has the Reverend Al Sharpton carried this burden of leadership? During the Tawana Brawley debacle the Reverend was found guilty of defamation and ordered to pay a financial fine. The Reverend Sharpton has also played it loose and free with his moral values. Many believe that we should not pay attention to our political leader's moral indiscretions, but in the black community most of the so called black leaders choose to accept the title of reverend which means that they represent a higher power, thus their personal affairs are our business. The Reverend Sharpton allegedly had an extramarital affair that led to a messy divorce. The Reverend has denied the affair, but black columnist Errol Louis of the New York Daily News notes that both Sharpton and Harris split from their spouses around the same time and traveled around the country together during Sharpton's presidential campaign. Louis was intrigued by the report that Harris "lives in a swanky Trump Place apartment and sports top-drawer toys like Mercedes, a mink coat and a $7000.00 Rolex."(Kincaid 1)

Ironically, the Village Voice claimed that Sharpton revealed in 2001 that Rev. Jackson was involved in an extramarital affair and had an illegitimate child. Jackson was discredited, at least for a while, enabling Sharpton to emerge as a national black spokesman, with enormous access to the national media. (Kincaid 1)

The Reverend Al Sharpton's lack of integrity has not been confined to his personal life; his presidential campaign was riddled with allegations of financial irregularities. In May of 2004 the Federal Election Commission ordered Sharpton to return $ 100,000.00 that he had received in federal matching funds for his presidential campaign. The ruling was in response to a complaint filed by the National Legal and Policy Center, which had noted "massive irregularities in the financing of his campaign." (Kincaid 1)

Sharpton continued with his financial improprieties The Voice reported that the Democratic National Committee paid Sharpton $ 86,715 in travel and consulting fees to compensate for his campaigning for John Kerry and other candidates. (Kincaid 1) It was also reported that The Reverend received a $15,000 fee for political consulting A.k.a. getting out the black vote.

Many question how much money Al Sharpton has been able to raise from private donation, from everyday American people. It is documented on the Individual Contributions of $ 200.00 or more to Presidential Pre Nomination Campaigns by State of The Contributor that Al Sharpton only raised $150,650.00 this shows that he has a very low level of support among the people. If one was to look at the Sharpton campaign they would have found the Reverend staying in $3000.00 a night hotels while his staff could have taken up residence in Las Vegas. One must wonder was this truly a presidential campaign or was it just an expensive country wide vacation for Al and his friends?

Because of his brash behavior Al Sharpton is viewed as a clown, much like the minstrels of the past. His political views follow the theory that blacks can do nothing without the help of the federal government. He supports big government and opposes tax cuts. He campaigns to enlarge a government that he claims has treated the black race unfairly. He supports taking more money out of our pockets because he believes that the government can spend our money better than we can.

The Reverend Al Sharpton along with the other so called black leaders have abandoned everything that Dr. Martin Luther King Jr. and Malcolm X lived and died for. If we are to continue to follow the path that they have laid for us we as a race will continue down this road of destruction that we find ourselves on. We need leaders with the moral authority and the intestinal fortitude to lead us on the difficult path back to the greatness of our potential, instead of justification of our weaknesses. There is a brighter day ahead it just isn't on the path that Al Sharpton would lead us on.

Julian Bond:

Horace Julian Bond was born January 14, 1940, in Nashville Tennessee. The son of educators, Julian has been a highly educated and articulate force for civil rights reform. The once crown prince of the civil rights movement Julian at every occasion will remind the masses that he walked with King, yet much of his promise has gone unfulfilled. What are the reasons that this capable and intelligent black politician has failed in his rise as a so called Black Leader

Julian Bond while attending Morehouse College involved himself in civil rights actions. Julian along with Ella Baker, Stokley Carmichael, and Bernice Reagon formed The Student Non-Violent Coordinating Committee. Julian also was involved in a sit in intended to desegregate Atlanta's lunch counters.

Julian was heavily involved in many civil rights actions and caught the attention of civil rights leaders including Dr. Martin Luther King Jr... Dr. King was briefly one of Bond's professors at Morehouse College and was the key plaintiff in the case which secured Bond's seat in the Georgia Legislature.

Unlike the other so called black leaders Julian Bond actually has been elected to office. Bond was the youngest person ever to achieve a seat in the Georgia Legislature. This feat was not without controversy. In 1965 Julian won a seat in the Georgia Legislature but statements by him condemning the Vietnam War and accusing the United State of violating international law, prompted the legislature to refuse admitting him. He was twice re-elected by voters in his district, but each time he was barred by the legislature. In 1966 the U.S. Supreme Court ruled his exclusion unconstitutional. Bond was sworn in on January 9, 1967, he served in the Georgia Legislature from 1967-1975 and in the Georgia Senate from 1975-1987.

How would one view Julian Bond's association with Dr. King? Most of us would think that Julian Bond looked up to Dr. King and believed in the movement, but many things that Bond has said would lead us to believe different.

Julian Bond was a mere teenager during the beginning of Dr. King's ascension as thee civil rights leader. In a January 20, 2003 interview by John Whitehead Bond stated

BOND: *"I grew up in a movement tradition that was hostile to the idea of the charismatic leader, the great figure who swoops in from out of town and says a few words at a mass meeting or leads a march and then swoops away, and the whole situation is changed. I was taught early on to be hostile to that idea. I really think that idea was detrimental to the development of a democratic movement.*

WHITEHEAD: *Is this how you saw DR. King*

BOND: *Oh very much so.*

This quote by Julian Bond illuminates his inability to see Dr. King's work as the unifying force for the black community that it was. We have been critical of the so called black leaders that tried to piece together the civil rights movement post Dr King for their lack of direction and the changing course of black unity. Julian Bond never seemed to be a true believer of how Dr. King ran his organization. In the same interview Bond states:

BOND: *King was surrounded by people who were nothing but yes men and said yes to everything he said he almost never heard real critiques to anything he said.*

WHITEHEAD: *do you think that if you had been one of his assistants you would have criticized him.*

BOND: *I probably would have been one of the yes men.*

Is it not obvious left with leaders such as Julian Bond why the civil rights movement imploded after the death of Dr. King and

Malcolm X, men of conviction and vision? Like Judas asking Christ when will you establish your kingdom here on earth, Julian Bond seems to be one who hung around to reap the benefits of being close to a true leader.

BOND: *We tend to think that every black minister in the south was engaged in the movement in fact only a small minority of the black clergy was involved it is a big mistake to think that every black minister from every pulpit was leading the charge. King and Abernathy and a small group around them were a very small minority.*

Julian Bond fails to understand the role that the black church played in the unity of the civil rights movement. Dr. King's strategy involved overcoming the unrighteousness of segregation with the righteousness of religion. Dr. King didn't instill faith in those who followed him he used the faith that was already there as fuel for the movement, and depended on the Christian conscious of those in power to finally do what was right.

Thanks to secular leaders like Julian Bond morality is no longer the norm. Blacks are being pushed further away from our traditional conservative values which are replaced by the reckless abandonment and lawlessness of a liberal philosophy.

Different from the civil rights leaders of the 1960's Julian Bond seemed to have little faith in the religious direction that was implemented by Dr. King (Christianity) or Malcolm X (Islam). He saw the NAACP as the answer to the ills of the black community. In 1968 Julian Bond became the first chairman of the NAACP.

The NAACP was created in 1909 by the merger of the Niagara Group, a group of young blacks led by W. E. B. Dubois, and three white republicans. This is the true story of the NAACP that was never taught in school. The three white republicans, Mary White Ovington, Oswald Garrison Villard, and William English Walling their intent was to be the front line of legal defense challenging bigotry in the American courts. Supported financial by many white abolitionists the NAACP became the biggest and most powerful weapon blacks had against racial discrimination. They open many doors and genuinely made a measurable difference in the quality of life of black Americans.

The NAACP's original mission was to stop the lynching of black citizens by the white Democrats that had regained power in the south after the failure of reconstruction.

Today under the leadership of Julian Bond the NAACP isn't a fraction of what it once was. Today the NAACP is a typical leftist, socialist, anti-American pawn of the Democratic Party.

What is the current state of such a proud and righteous organization under Julian Bond's leadership? The current state is that it is no longer interested in the advancement of people of color, but is invested only in the advancement of a liberal philosophy. Proof of this is his stand against such prominent and accomplished conservative black leaders such as Clarence Thomas, J.C. Watts, and Condoleezza Rice.

How would Dr. King have handled those on the opposing political side of himself? Would he have tried to find some common ground, or would he have tried to destroy them? Julian Bond has not only been critical of these black conservative politicians, but has brought into question their vary blackness. Insults such as Uncle Tom and puppets of the Republican Party are frequently heard when Bond speaks. Julian Bond is of the belief if you don't follow the Democratic Party then you are not for the Blackman. Thankfully W.E.B. Dubois didn't agree with this when he merged his organization with three white Republicans to create the very organization that Julian Bond now uses as a weapon to destroy and defame any black not beholden to the liberals.

Julian Bond makes it a habit to refer to black conservatives as puppets or Uncle Tom's, and as bad as that is, let's view how he handled the announcement of Condoleezza Rice being awarded the NAACP Image Award. Julian was so upset that he asked then NAACP President Kwasi Mfume to tender his resignation. In spite of the fact when Mfume took over the organization in 1996 the NAACP was reeling from sexual harassment charges filed on his predecessor along with being investigated by the IRS and being 3.2 million dollars in debt and the organizations tax exempt status being challenged. Mfume turned the organization around bringing it back from controversy and near bankruptcy. Yet, none of this mattered; Mfume had crossed the line by recognizing the accomplishments of a conservative black woman.

Mfume also, in Bond's eye's, was guilty for trying to reach out to the Republican Party. Mfume saw that there were certain issues such as school vouchers and supporting faith based organizations that they agreed with the current Republican administration. Mfume also saw that the black voters did themselves a disservice with their blind support of the Democratic Party. Mfume recognized that the black voters could position themselves in a better bartering position if each party felt there was a possibility to gain the black vote. As it stood the Democrats, feeling that blacks always have and always will support them, have no need to concern themselves with black issues after election time. With the Republican Party receiving no more than 10% of the black vote, many felt it a waste of resources to attempt to court the black vote. This new and different approach by Mfume enraged Chairman Bond. With Mfume first supporting Condoleezza Rice and then reaching out for common ground with the Republican Party the rift between Bond and Mfume became unmendable.

One is left wondering what the true mission of the NAACP is. Is the true mission the advancement of people of color, or is it the advancement of the Democratic Party's agenda. As we document in the following chapter, the accomplishments of Secretary of State Condoleezza Rice are the realization of Dr. Martin Luther King's dream, a country where a black woman from the south could rise to the heights in our government on her ability. Yet, Julian Bond found it an offense to nominate such a qualified individual for recognition of her accomplishments. Bond even countered her nomination for the award by nominating "Boondocks" cartoonist Aaron McGruder for the Image award. McGruder had gained Bond's favor because of his history of ridicule of Secretary Rice. McGruder even went as far as calling the Secretary a murderer for her role in the war in Iraq.

These types of characterizations of Republicans are much more to the liking of Chairman Bond. During a speech at the Ernest N. Morial Convention Center in New Orleans Chairman Bond proclaimed that President George W. Bush has "selected political nominees from the Taliban wing of American politics, appeased the wretched appetites of the extreme right wing and chosen cabinet officials whose devotion to the confederacy is nearly canine in its uncritical affection. (Williams p1)

During a 2003 appearance at the National Press Club, Bond referred to the Republican Party "as a crazed swarm of right wing locust' that have sought to "subvert, ignore, defy and destroy the laws that require an America which is bias-free. Later that night Bond dubbed the Republicans, "the white people's party." (Williams p1)

Bond like other so called black leaders buy into the lies told to the black race by the Democratic Party. They have been purchased by the promise of preference by politicians that pay them attention only during election time. They value their own rise to power over the progression of those who they claim to serve. They disregard the methods that have been successful in the past for unfulfilled promises of the American left.

Finally Mfume suggested sending a letter to President Bush, mapping out ways that they could work together to help the community. Bond rejected the idea. Mfume being genuinely concerned with improving the status of his people sent the letter anyway. For this gesture of peace and willingness to work with Republicans, Bond had Mfume voted out. Bond sent a clear message that there is no room within the NAACP for intellectual diversity, only loyal servitude to the Democratic Party. (Williams p1)

Julian Bond has used hate rhetoric as a tool to scare the black race into a single minded following of a philosophy that has not served us well. I often question what is it that leaders like Bond see in the Democratic Party? Being an intelligent man I wonder why he never stumbled across the information presented in this book. Why he has never remembered that the fight for civil rights in the south was fought against the Democratic Party. It makes me wonder what his objectives are when he fails to acknowledge high achievement that should be used as a motivating force within the black community, instead of following the party line and acting as their attack dog barking out liberal talking points.

With Julian Bond's unwillingness to recognize the truth we must question whether he is able to lead us to the place that we as a people need to be. Julian Bond has taken a once great organization, the NAACP, and turned it into a partisan weapon of the Democratic Party, and Julian Bond is their number one hammer.

Summary:

The so called black leaders that took over the reigns of the civil rights movement chose to move the black race in a different direction than the successful leaders of the 1960's. Many of these leaders currently receive compensation from Democratic organization to carry the liberal banner and act as pied pipers leading the black voters to the polls on Election Day. One must question were these practices in action during the important turning point of the 1960's. We have presented the evidence that many lies have been told to vilify the Republican Party and present the Democratic Party as champions of civil rights. One must question how could we have been so deceived?

The answer to this question is not favorable to the leaders highlighted in this chapter. It is obvious that they worked with the very Democratic officials that denied our rights. They assisted in rewriting history concerning who supported blacks through their struggle to achieve our civil rights. Like Judas they have been well paid with cash and status, but what price has been paid by those who followed. In order to protect their status as leaders, our black leaders have refused to listen to opposing views, and have vilified members of their own race who don't agree with the path taken by black Americans. This policy of closed mindedness has cost the black race a heavy price. Many blacks have listened to our current leaders and fed on the hate filled lies told only to be left dependent on a government unable to satisfy their needs.

These same leaders that attack anyone with different ideas continue to lead the black race on the road that has degraded our communities for more than forty years. It is time we look for new leaders with new ideas and that follow a different philosophy. How much longer can we afford to follow ineffective leaders?

In the next chapter we present black leaders of the Republic Party, leaders who believe that success for the black race will be found on a different road.

CHAPTER 7

BLACK REPUBLICANS

Since the 1960's, when Dr. Martin Luther King Jr. delivered the black vote to the Democratic Party in protest of Barry Goldwater's nomination for President by the Republican Party, blacks have aligned themselves with the Democratic Party. The democrats have cleverly rewritten history to identify republicans as those who fought the advancement of the civil rights movement. This has caused a mistrust and hatred of republicans by black Americans. When in truth, the most violent and racist acts committed from the days of reconstruction, the enactment of Jim Crow, and the protest of the twentieth century civil rights movement were perpetrated by the hands of democratic officials. Democrats committed such acts as fire hosing of black civil rights protestors by Bull Conner, to blocking black students from integrating white schools by George McGovern. Yet, somehow history has been twisted to portray the Democratic Party as the sole champions of civil rights. Nothing could be further from the truth.

President Lyndon B. Johnson signed into law the Civil Rights Act of 1964, which was originally started by President John F. Kennedy. This was done over a filibuster led by the Democratic Senator from Tennessee, Al Gore Sr., and the majority of the "no" votes coming from the Southern Democrats. President Johnson himself voted against the majority of civil rights legislation while serving as a senator from Texas. Yet today, any black person who claims the Republican Party is considered to be a turncoat, an uncle tom, or one who has forgotten his roots. Black Republicans, such as Justice Clarence Thomas have been attacked and called tokens or had their blackness questioned because they believe that the conservative path will better serve the black community.

Ostracizing black conservatives is not reserved for those in public office. Any black person who dares to go against the status quo will have their blackness questioned. Different from most black conservatives I know, I have always identified with the conservative philosophy. I didn't start out as a democrat and then see the light. I have always been confused that the majority of black America is unable to see that the Republican Party better represents the core values and beliefs held in the black community. Most blacks have been fooled by the lies that democratic politicians have told to play on the fears of the black community and to secure their vote come election time.

During the 2004 Presidential election a pro-democratic group created ads showing black civil rights protestors from the 1960's being fire hosed. This ad stated "This is how republicans use to keep blacks from voting". Blacks need to realize the truth that this act was perpetrated by democrats. Yet the democrats continue to use lies such as this to cast a false image of racism on the Republican Party.

In this chapter we will examine several prominent black conservatives. We will examine what it is about Conservatism that makes them believe that this is the correct path for all Americans.

It's time to live what you teach

One day, during a chemistry study session, a girl, who knew I was writing a book about black conservatism, asked me if I was attending the lecture at Syracuse University by Congressman J.C. Watts. At the time I was totally unaware that one of my favorite politicians was coming to Syracuse.

I had just recently started college after being laid off from the job that I spent the last fourteen years working at. I had received about a year notification that layoffs were definite. Faced with trying to find a job in the technical field that I worked in, and taking a major salary cut starting at a new company, I sat down and discussed with my wife the possibility of going to college. I had followed conservative politics for years, the first president I had voted for was President Ronald Regan, but now it was time to put some of my conservative ideas into action. So with some discussion my wife and I decide to pay our bills down, as much as we could, and I would attend school full time.

One of the greatest blessings that a man can receive from God is a good wife. In this I am the luckiest man in the world. In modern times it is rare to find women willing to work to exhaustion so that her husband can go to school full time and truly concentrating on doing well. In this my wife is on the top of the list. We as a family see my returning to school as an investment for our future. I in return have been able to concentrate on my studies and have received such honors as acceptance to Phi Theta Kappa and acceptance to the 2004 National Dean's List.

Now I tell this story because I was laid off from work after the 911 terrorist bombings, and like many others who lost their jobs during this time period I could have blamed the current Republican Administration. I just couldn't see things that way. I saw being laid off as a blessing in that I now had the chance to go to school and reach my potential. Many times in the past I had opportunities to go to school, but with the responsibilities of a family, sometimes it's hard to take that first step. Besides I have always had an entrepreneur's spirit. I have always dreamed about owning my own business. My wife makes nursing scrubs and sells them to her co-workers, and I tried my hand at running small auto detailing shops. My co-writer Eric and I have tried many different business ventures through the years, none that have produced the level of success that we dreamed of, yet we still try.

Getting laid off and being forced to tighten our belts has reaffirmed some important conservative values for me. I must admit that I have not been the best fiscal conservative. Being raised in a middle class family that did quite well, I have always had things that I desired within my grasp. My father didn't spoil us, we had to work and earn anything above and beyond basic sustenance. Having to work for the extras in life taught me a valuable lesson, that all things are attainable. I remember purchasing my first car when I was seventeen. I worked two jobs during the summer, one working as a printer in the school print shop from 7:00 in the morning until 3:00 in the afternoon, and then I bused tables at the Red Lobster from 4:30 until close. It was a rough summer, but it all seemed worth it when I was driving that 1976 Plymouth Sports Fury.

I have always believed that hard work produces results, and marrying a woman from the Philippines I have to catch my breath to keep up with her. She has been blessed with the best work ethics I have ever seen. I think that because she comes from an impoverished country she is able to recognize opportunity. Yet, sometimes she and I have got caught up in chasing material wealth instead of saving for the future.

Our current situation has woken us up to the error of our ways, and we now try to live within our means. We look ahead to a bright future because this is truly the land of opportunity. After I finish school and return to work my wife plans to go to school to further her education, because she has seen the difference that a higher education is making in my life.

Congressman J.C. Watts

As I left school that day I frantically called my co-writer and friend Eric. " J.C. Watts is speaking at Syracuse University tonight, we have to go! Congressman Watts was lecturing as part of his book tour. He was a politician that I had watched closely, being that he was a black conservative I felt that I had a connection with him because we both saw that conservatism would be beneficial to the black race. Eric and I had planed to include a section in the book we were writing about black conservatives, and what a great opportunit; this would be to hear Congressman Watts speak. Maybe I could even negotiate a short interview for the book.

That night listening to Congressman Watts speak, I heard the best presentation of the conservative message that I had ever heard. He spoke on the importance of family, religion, fiscal responsibilities, school choice, tax cuts and many other subjects' dear to my heart. Afterwards we waited in line for about forty-five minutes in order to have him sign the book that he was promoting. We purposely positioned ourselves towards the end of the line so as to have more time to talk to the former Congressman. Upon meeting him and finding out we shared the same first name we had a great conversation where we were able to tell him of the book we were working on. He graciously offered his resources in assisting us on our project. I didn't try to muscle an interview that night I wanted to respect his time limitation, but I got something better than an interview that night. I purchased his book, What Color Is a Conservative My life in Politics. This book gives a clear story of who he is and how he arrived where he is. The following information is from that book

Congressman J. C. Watts was born in Eufaula, Oklahoma. Born Julius Caesar Watts Jr., son of Buddy and Helen Watts, He was blessed with a close knit family that had the support of extended family and friends. Congressman Watts formed his values on family from a strong hardworking father that didn't allow barriers like The Great Depression and racism stop him from his hunt for the American dream. I would venture to say that the strong conservative family values that Congressman Watts supports for this country comes from a blessed upbringing where he learned the value of a dollar along with the benefits of hard work.

Congressman Watts is a throw back to great civil rights leaders of the past. His strong foundation in the church and his understanding of traditional family values is the type of message that we in the black community need to hear. With all conservatives his stance against the expansion of the welfare state has gotten him labeled as a turncoat. Congressman Watts has stayed consistent in his belief that welfare is a poison that is killing the black race. He supports a message of self-reliance that he was raised on and that has brought him success in life.

While reading through Congressmen Watt's book I felt such a connection with him. Many of our life experiences are different, him being a nationally recognized football star and congressman and me just an above average black American. I feel that, like the majority of black America we both were raised with similar values. These values, which derived from the church, are the thing that connects all black people in this country. So whether rich or poor, famous sports legend or high school football star we in the black community are eternally connected.

When I read about Congressman Watt's beliefs and how he experienced an awakening about his political beliefs I too believe that the majority of black America would experience this would they take an honest look at their beliefs and which political philosophy follows those beliefs.

The one thing that I respect most about Congressman Watts is the one thing that has cost the conservative movement the most. Congressman Watts pushed for term limits. He believes that politics should not be a life long career. Term limits was never passed. Yet Congressman Watts showed true character in imposing term limits on himself. When you truly believe in something, you don't need a law to follow it; you just have to know that it's right. Congressman Watts served this country honorable for three terms in The House of Representatives. He was the first black American in a leadership position from the Republican Party since reconstruction. Yet, with all his accomplishments most blacks will say that he was a token. He was used as an attempt to fool black Americans into thinking that the Republican Party is no longer the racist party that we all know that they are.

Like other black republicans J.C. Watts is the best at what he does. His countless successes and his failures that he showed the strength to recover from, have made him into a man that all should respect. His life experiences, that are no different than most of black America, have given him insight on how to improve the nation for everyone. This is another great distinction that sets Congressman Watts apart from other black politicians. He looks to serve all races. When he speaks, he speaks of a better day for all Americans. He follows the true dream of our great civil rights leader Dr. Martin Luther King Jr. That one-day we all, black and white could sit down at the table and share in the fruits of a great nation.

Secretary of State Dr. Condoleezza Rice

White House photo by Tina Hager

As a black American, one of the key elements that continue to draw me to the conservative philosophy is the quality of the black representatives of conservatism. Dr. Condoleezza Rice is an excellent representation of this. She is one of the most accomplished and truly qualified persons on today's political scene. Yet, like all other black conservatives Dr. Rice has had her blackness called into question. Many prominent members of the 1960's civil rights movement question how such an intelligent black woman could offer her service to the Republican Party.

Dr. Condoleezza Rice was born November 14, 1954 in Birmingham, Alabama; a town that she once refereed to as "Bombingham" because of all the bombings that took place there during the civil rights movement. Dr Rice was no stranger to the terrors that took place during the civil rights movement. She was best friends with one of the four little girls that died in the famous bombing of a church in Birmingham. Condoleezza was the only child to Rev. John Rice, a minister and a school guidance counselor, and Angelena Rice, a teacher. Unlike Dr. King, Dr. Rice's family did not publicly participate in the 1960's civil rights demonstrations. Like many other blacks of the time, the Rice family believed in other methods in order to gain our equality.

Condoleezza's parents raised her to follow the true path of success in this country, education. Dr. Rice earned her bachelor's degree in political science, cum laude and Phi Beta Kappa, from the University of Denver in 1974; her master's from the University of Notre Dame in 1975; and her Ph.D. from the Graduate School of International Studies at the University of Denver in 1981. She is a Fellow of the American Academy of Arts and Sciences, and has been awarded honorary doctorates from Morehouse College in 1991, the University of Alabama in 1994, the University of Notre Dame in 1995, the National Defense University in 2002, the Mississippi College School of Law in 2003, the University of Louisville and Michigan State University in 2004(National 1).

As professor of political science, Dr. Rice has been on the Stanford faculty since 1981 and has won two of the highest teaching honors -- the 1984 Walter J. Gores Award for Excellence in Teaching and the 1993 School of Humanities and Sciences Dean's Award for Distinguished Teaching (National 1).

At Stanford, she has been a member of the Center for International Security and Arms Control, a Senior Fellow of the Institute for International Studies, and a Fellow (by courtesy) of the Hoover Institution. Her books include Germany Unified and Europe Transformed (1995) with Philip Zelikow, The Gorbachev Era (1986) with Alexander Dallin and Uncertain Allegiance: The Soviet Union and the Czechoslovak Army (1984). She also has written numerous articles on Soviet and East European foreign and defense policy, and has addressed audiences in settings ranging from the U.S. Ambassador's Residence in Moscow to the Commonwealth Club to the 1992 and 2000 Republican National Conventions (National 1).

From 1989 through March 1991, the period of German reunification and the final days of the Soviet Union, she served in the Bush Administration as Director, and then Senior Director, of Soviet and East European Affairs in the National Security Council, and a Special Assistant to the President for National Security Affairs. In 1986, while an international affairs fellow of the Council on Foreign Relations, she served as Special Assistant to the Director of the Joint Chiefs of Staff. In 1997, she served on the Federal Advisory Committee on Gender -- Integrated Training in the Military. She was a member of the boards of directors for the Chevron Corporation, the Charles Schwab Corporation, the William and Flora Hewlett Foundation, the University of Notre Dame, the International Advisory Council of J.P. Morgan and the San Francisco Symphony Board of Governors. She was a Founding Board member of the Center for a New Generation, an educational support fund for schools in East Palo Alto and East Menlo Park, California and was Vice President of the Boys and Girls Club of the Peninsula. In addition, her past board service has encompassed such organizations as Transamerica Corporation, Hewlett Packard, the Carnegie Corporation, Carnegie

Endowment for International Peace, The Rand Corporation, the National Council for Soviet and East European Studies, the Mid-Peninsula Urban Coalition and KQED, public broadcasting for San Francisco (National 1).

Dr. Rice is the realization of Dr. Martin Luther King's dream. That a black woman born in the south during the height of the civil rights movement could rise to the level of being the first black woman to serve as both National Security Advisor and Secretary of State.

This black woman is the example that we as black Americans should be celebrating and listening to. While many discount her achievements and claim that she is a token for the Republican Party to hold up as an argument against their so-called racist policies. Does that not minimize all that she has accomplished? Does that not take away from the years of hard work that Dr. Rice did to position her where she is today? During Her conformation hearings in front of the U.S. Senate I sat shocked while Democratic Senators called her qualifications into question. I listened to radio interviews where our so-called black leaders repeated that Dr. Rice is not representative of the black community. To those statements I respond, what more could you look for in a leader?

Unlike the black leadership of today Dr. Rice comes with an impressive resume that proves her abilities. She should be exulted as a shining example of what a black Americans can achieve in this country instead of attacked as the President's flunky. It is obvious to those who care to look that Dr. Rice is one of President's Bush's most trusted advisors, and most important has the qualification to do so. How much further could we as a race of people progress if we would select role models like Dr. Rice? Role models that are successful, accomplished, qualified, and like the leaders of the past God fearing.

Dr. Rice is a prime example that the Republican Party is following what Dr. King dreamed of "judging a person by the content of their character, and not the color of their skin. I remember seeing a newspaper article that was a response to a statement made by the NAACP that President's Bush's White House had a "DO NOT ENTER" sign for blacks. Why do we as black Americans continue to buy into this type of rhetoric when we have such impressive black representation within the Republican Party? We have followed the principles of Liberalism since the late 1960's, yet look at the success of those that have chosen a different path like Dr. Rice. Black Americans need to ask themselves where we want to go, and is the message that we are getting from or current leadership going to get us there.

Ambassador Alan Keyes

When we look inside the black community for qualified pe to lead, we need to look no further than Alan Keyes. Truly of the most overlooked resources of brilliance, Alan Keyes a unique understanding of the constitution and how it appl modern times. His unwavering support for the principles t this country was founded on has him recognized as the mo formidable defender of America's founding principles in today's political Arena.

Ambassador Alan Keyes is an eleven-year veteran of the U.S. State Department. He served in the U.S. Foreign Services and on the staff of the National Security Council. From 1983-1985 he served as President Ronald Regan's, ambassador to the United Nations Economic and Social Council, where he represented the interests of the United States in the United Nations General Assembly. In 1985 he was appointed Assistant Secretary of State for International Organizations where he served honorably from 1985-1988.

Like other prominent black conservatives Ambassador Keyes followed the path of education in order to find equality. Alan Keyes, has a Ph.D. in government from Harvard University, and wrote his dissertation on constitutional theory. The ambassador is multi talented to include speaking fluent French, and has studied Spanish, Russian, and ancient Greek. He has authored several books to include *Masters of the Dream: The strength and Betrayal of Black America.*

Alan Keyes, unlike our so-called black leadership, believes in the constitution and the principles that this country was founded upon. His unrivaled understanding of the constitution has led him to follow policies and principles that would return this country and the black community to the moral path that once made us great. He is a true conservative, and has championed such issues as the unalienable rights and biblical truth in defense of the unborn. Keyes has called for the abolishment of abortion from our land and eloquently represents how this policy of killing the unborn is not constitutional and has opened the door for the moral decay that is rampant in the United States.

Alan Keyes, in regard to the political priorities of this nation, is a refreshing change from the self-serving dishonest politics of destruction that has become the norm. He believes that we need to strengthen the foundations of political liberty in America. He believes that the people need to take back control of our government. He believes that the sole purpose of government is to secure our unalienable rights promised to each one of us by the constitution.

Alan Keyes recognizes the moral decay that is taking place in our communities, and calls for the return to biblical guidance for or government as the answer to our problems. Because of his understanding of the constitution he understands that the separation of church and state doctrine is a misinterpretation of the constitution. He states that The First Amendment prohibition of established religion aims at forbidding all government sponsored coercion of religious conscience. It does not forbid all religious influence upon politics or society. Our so-called black politicians that refuse to insist to a return to biblical guidance. They claim to be believers in the Word of God and the moral standards that made us the nation we once were, yet they are unwilling to proclaim the need for God's presence in our national decision making. Alan Keyes has refused to succumb to organization like the A.C.L.U. in order to gain political favor, and he also has refused to adopt political views that are seemingly more popular in modern times, yet will lead us to destruction.

Alan Keyes' fresh ideas on replacing the income tax with a national sales tax, is a policy that would positively impact the black community. Yet, because of his misunderstood views on programs such as welfare and affirmative action, most discount him and fail to uncover the brilliance that he posses.

We in the black community need to demand higher standards for our leaders. We need integrate the standards that we hold dear in our spiritual lives with what we demand politically. We need to look to those such as Alan Keyes, who are men and women of unquestionable moral standards and those who understand the importance of family and limited role of government. . Men and women who understand that no government program can fix the ills of our communities, but only through a return to biblical guidance can we hope to recapture our young from social deviance.

The one important truth that the liberal philosophy fails to recognize is that the Bible was the blueprint for our constitutions. All throughout the document that guarantees our rights as citizens are references back to the divine word of God. It is God who grants us our freedoms. This was the intention of our founding fathers, and to try to remove God from our government is to remove the very foundation that this country was built on.

Men and women, such as Alan Keyes, understand and are willing to implement the proper role of God in our political decisions. We as Bible believing Christians in the black community need to support Alan Keyes, and politicians like him. For if we don't, we leave our destiny in the hands of those who seek to remove God and his blessings from this nation.

JUSTICE CLARENCE THOMAS

Justice Clarence Thomas is probably one of the most controversial black conservatives on today's political scene. Justice Thomas is so detested that liberals spared no expense in fighting his appointment to the Supreme Court. What is it about his beliefs that caused such fear and hatred of this black man born in the grips of racist Georgia? What possible view did he hold that incited liberals to defame his character and permanently mark him as an enemy to the black community?

Justice Clarence Thomas was born June 23, 1948 in the Pinpoint community near Savannah Georgia. Born during the Jim Crow Era, he is no stranger to racism and the debilitating affect it had on the black race. Justice Thomas started out his higher education at Conception Seminary later transferring to Holy Cross College where he graduated A.B. cum laude. Alpha Sigma Nu, Purple Key, and then attended Yale Law School.

Justice Thomas always held the belief that blacks are equal, that we only needed to be given an equal chance. Growing up under the restrictions of segregation had an enlightening affect on him. That no man, black or white should be treated unfairly. During his stay at Holy Cross he flirted with black militancy. He was the only Black Student Union member to vote against establishing an all-black dorm corridor (Fletcher A01).

Clarence Thomas was admitted to the Bar in 1974, his government service includes Assistant Attorney General of Missouri, Legislative assistant to Senator John C. Danforth, Assistant Secretary for Civil Rights, U.S Department of Education, and Chairman U.S. Equal Employment Opportunity Commission. His judicial offices include U.S. Court of Appeals for the District of Columbia Circuit, and an Associate Justice of the United States Supreme Court.

Not unlike other black conservatives Justice Thomas comes with a plethora of qualification. His stance on Affirmative Action has been a source of contention between him and the so-called black leadership. Justice Thomas' opposition to affirmative action is that it is demeaning to minorities and problematic under the constitution. Concerning affirmative action Justice Thomas in 1987 wrote " I think that preferential hiring on the basis of race or gender will increase racial divisiveness, disempower women and minorities by fostering the notion they are permanently disabled and in need of handouts" (Fletcher A01). Writing in a concurrence to a 1995 ruling establishing tougher standards for justifying federal affirmative action programs, Thomas said:" So-called benign discrimination teaches many that because of chronic and immutable handicaps, minorities cannot compete with them without their patronizing indulgence" (Fletcher A01).

Because of his different views on programs that have been viewed by the majority of blacks as helpful, Justice Thomas has always been viewed as the enemy when in truth he holds the beliefs that the black race would progress further without a program that labels them as inferior. This view is held by the majority of conservatives yet, is often mistaken for racism.

Since Justice Thomas' appointment to the Supreme Court he has earned the image as a hard line holdout. Justice Thomas's belief in the constitution and adherence to it has allied him with the conservative icon Antonin Scalia. Because of Thomas's silence during oral argument and his similar voting record with Justice Scalia many have perceived Justice Thomas as a puppet to the senior Justice Scalia. Nothing could be further from the truth. Justice Thomas states "People say that because I'm black, Justice Scalia does my work for me, but I rarely see him, so he must have a chip in my brain" (Fletcher A01). Justices Thomas and Scalia vote alike to a degree of 92 percent of the time. But what of past Justices with similar voting records such as Justice Thurgood Marshall and his liberal court comrade, William J. Brennan.They voted together 94 percent of the time according to the Michigan State data which records judicial voting history (Fletcher A01). This similar voting record never earned any derogatory statements for the first black Supreme Court Justice. Could it be because he held liberal views that such things went unnoticed?

Justice Thomas has held steadfast to the conservative philosophy. A philosophy that he maintains will lead the black race out of poverty, and to prosperity. If one looks at where following liberalism has gotten the black race, one might find that it is time for a change. Is conservatism the change that is needed? Can the black race open their eyes and see that those who carry the conservative banner are those that are the protectors of what we as black people claim to cherish.

Justice Janice Rogers Brown

California Supreme Court Justice Janice Rogers Brown has waited two years for a confirmation vote from the Senate for her appointment to the Federal Appellate Court by President Bush. She is one of many judges entrenched in the secular –vs- faith battles within the United States Senate.

A battle has emerged in the United States Senate. We as blacks need to decided which sided we will support. The liberal wing of the Democratic Party has started a war against the confirmation of any judge that claims religious belief. Judges such as Janice Rogers Brown, face punishment from secularist for their beliefs. After a two-year wait a bitterly divided Senate committee voted along party lines to approve her nomination as a federal appellate court judge. But will she get the opportunity for the full Senate vote for confirmation promised to her by our constitution? Not if liberals like the Senator from New York, Chuck Shumer, have anything to say about it. The New York Senator has stated that they, the democrats, have a problem with judges who have "deeply held beliefs".

The black race must decide which side of the fence it will come down on. There are clearly drawn lines for this fight. Liberals unable to pass their agendas at the ballot box are now turning to the courts and rouge judges with no interest in upholding the constitution to inflict their unpopular, unconstitutional views upon us. Judges like Clarence Thomas and Janice Rogers Brown who do not believe in interpreting the law according to modern times, and who believe in strict adherence to the constitution are a threat to those on the left, those who believe that the constitution is a flexible document bending and changing to the winds of time.

This is not the first time that Liberals have looked to the courts to create laws outside the constitution. As we covered in chapter three the landmark case of Plessy –vs.– Ferguson in 1896, which created the segregation laws, was delivered upon us by The Supreme Court. Roe –

vs.– Wade that legalized abortion also delivered to us by The Supreme Court. Are we as black people ready to allow twelve individuals with lifetime appointments to write law for the United States? This is not what the constitution intended. Are we in the black race, who profess to be followers of Christ, prepared to side with the political philosophy which seeks to eliminate judges who hold "deeply held beliefs" from contention for seats on our courts. Judge Janice Rogers Brown recently stated "When we move away from that, (speaking of religious traditions) we change our whole conception of the most significant idea that America has to offer, which is this idea of human freedom and this notion of liberty".

The problems that liberals have with judges like Janice Rogers Brown and Clarence Thomas is not limited to their religious beliefs.

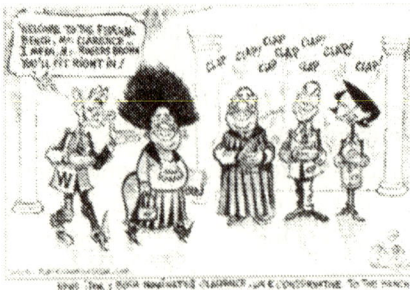

Reference this cartoon created by a black liberal organization called the Black Commentator. This cartoon was released in response to Janice Rogers Brown's appointment by President Bush. In the corresponding article it states that "Janice Brown is a Jim Crow-era judge, in black face. How interesting that they chose to use similar tactics that white racist of that era used to insult and demean blacks.

These Justices' views on civil rights issues have caused black liberals to leave no insult unsaid pertaining to these judges.

Yet, just as in any other thing that liberals choose to do; I guess it is O.K. when blacks do it to other blacks. Were it a white conservative using such tactics to make their point, the N.A.A.C.P., The Congressional Black Caucus, and every other liberal with the ability to read would be calling for someone's resignation. I personally am still insulted.

Black liberals opposing Justice Rogers state that because of her interpretation of the constitution concerning affirmative action that she is an enemy to the black race, and brand her a bootlicker to the Republican Party. What are Justice Roger's views on this issue? In the article from The Black Commentator they state that Justice Rogers believes that the constitution doesn't allow for affirmative action, but rather, equality of individual opportunity.

What was it that the great civil rights leader Dr. Martin Luther King Jr. sought for the black race? Was it not equal opportunity? The programs sought by today black liberal leaders are so far from what was fought for during the civil rights movement. Today's black leaders continue to view the black race as inferiors in need of government programs. Incapable of seizing the opportunity that is before us, not realizing that the very programs they seek continue to hold our race back. If a leader continuously tells his followers that we are not as capable and can not succeed with out his help, many will believe him.

But what about those of us who believe in our abilities, and seek only an equal opportunity for success, and see education as the great equalizer, are we wrong? What about those of us, who see programs such as affirmative action as a label for unequal ability, are we racist? It's time for the Black race to reevaluate the path we will take. We need to look at which political philosophy best serves us.

What does the liberal philosophy have to offer us? It is a universally held belief within the Christian church that we are all born spiritually dead, thus we have a hole inside us. In 1963 the Supreme Court stopped using the theory of *Divine Law* to interpret the constitution. Left with beliefs and void of any spiritual guidance we chose worldliness to fill that hole. Liberalism has no steadfast reference to determine right from wrong. It is guided by the emotion of what feels right for the time. Our founding fathers, in their great wisdom, chose Divine Law as the standard by which all decisions should be made. Because Divine Law is unwavering it gave us an unchanging measure of right from wrong. With liberalism we are left without. We are left with gray area. When you examine this, is it any wonder that our children are confused about right and wrong? Is it hard to believe that teenagers, with no respect for life, can walk into a school and slaughter their classmates and teachers? Left with only the world to fill that hole, it's not a big surprise.

Without a spiritual guide we as a society are left confused and divided on issues such as homosexual marriage. The gay rights lobby love to attach themselves to the civil rights movement in an attempt to create camaraderie with the black community. There are a few major problems with this view.

First homosexuality is a behavior. If we begin to justify behaviors then we open the door to all behaviors such as pedophilia, and even beastiality. Acts such as these are condemned in the Bible, but if we follow the liberal philosophy the winds of change may find a time when society accepts these acts as normal.

Second, the black race has been denied rights that were given to all U.S. citizens. This is different than the situation homosexuals find themselves in. Homosexuals believe that they are being denied the right of marriage, along with all the rights afforded married couples. Yet, in truth they have the same rights that each person of their gender has. A homosexual male has the same rights that a heterosexual male has. They both have the right to marry a woman. The homosexual male opposes this view stating, but I don't want to marry a woman. Is that not similar to a forty-year-old man stating that he wants to marry a thirteen-year-old girl? Our society has set up boundaries to what is right and wrong. Without a guide or a standard we are left to people's emotions and worldly desires to define what is acceptable. If we decide to follow that road, like powerful empires of the past, it will lead to our destruction.

The conservative message has held firm against legalizing homosexual marriage, because our standard, the word of God, states that marriage is between a man and a woman the only formula for procreation. Thus, conservatives are left with a choice. Serve God and hold firm to his commandments, or bend to the issue of the moment and go against God, I choose to serve God.

SUMMARY

When one looks at the black conservatives presented in this chapter it is evident that they represent the better part of the black community. The path they have taken is one that will lead the black race back to the dignified place that we once held. All of these prominent blacks have followed the path of education and hard work to find success in this country, and through finding success have much more to offer than the government nipple offered to us by our current black leadership. In a time that is so critical the black race can no longer afford to blindly follow the lies and patronizing acts that the liberals have given us since the late 1960's. We must open our eyes and decide will we follow those who follow Christ, or will we continue to buy the lies told us by the liberals that we are not as intelligent and thus in need of their government help? When will we as a race break that final link of slavery and decide that we are capable of success? Will we follow a message with the courage to tell us that the deviant path that many of us have chosen will lead to our destruction? Or will we listen to a philosophy void of God that discourages judgement of bad behavior and says it just a sign of the times?

As more and more young blacks follow the path of education, more are, with discerning eyes, able to see the lies told to us by the liberals. With the appointment of qualified blacks in national positions such as Secretary of State and Secretary of Education, more young blacks are opening their eyes and seeing that conservatism is better able to serve their needs. The truth that liberals have feared is rising to the surface. A new generation of educated blacks is coming that no longer accepts the liberal lies told to our ancestors, a generation willing and able to research the truth and not be swayed by the tales of the past.

CHAPTER 8

A LOOK IN THE MIRROR

"Black Like Me"

Black like me
Why can't they be, black like me?
Why don't they talk?
Why don't they walk?
Why don't they act like me?
They live by Ebonics & the
Ghetto way of life.
They think that without the ghetto they
Can't live, but that thought isn't right.
Our personalities are different, but our skin is
All brown, their parents raised them different, so
Their smiles are all frowns.
Or maybe that's just me, my mom, and my dad.
If I dare ask them this question, they'll surely get
mad. But I don't even bother because they're not
like me We don't talk; we don't walk the same
They're not black like me.

By: Ashley P. Brown

How insightful is this poem from a twelve-year-old black girl. It speaks of the ever-increasing division that is taking place in the Black Community. We as black people must wake up and see that the war between true black culture and urban culture is leading to the destruction of our race.

Why is it that black children define themselves with such negative labels? Why do we adopt negative terminology and try to attach a positive meaning to it?

In this chapter we will take a look in the mirror at how some things are in the black community. Only by being truthful about things do we have a chance to change them.

Through the difficult years of Jim Crow and the struggles of the Civil Rights movement Black Americans kept their dignity. The struggles that we all faced as a people united us to a common cause. The goal of the Black Community was to assimilate into a society and share in the opportunities that this country offered. In our pursuit to assimilate we had our priorities in proper order. We loved the church and looked to it for strength and guidance, we respected the law for we knew we would not receive a fair shake in the courts, and we followed the true path of success, education. During these times, parents pushed their children to achieve. Even though society said that we were less, this false message was never passed on in the home. In my family like many others, each generation tried to progress further than the one before them. My Grandfather only attended to the eleventh grade but he encouraged all his children to graduate high school. My father graduated from college and he encouraged all his children to attend college. This was a popular theme in the black community; take it a step further than your parents.
We were a moral people because we were well grounded in the church and received our morality from a higher source.

The changes of the late sixties and the early seventies set the black race on a different course. The volatility of the Civil Rights movement and the assassination of our two most prominent civil rights leaders set the black race on an anti-social path. We lost the true message of the civil rights movement. The Black Panthers started out as a positive group with a message of hope and self-reliance. But they quickly turned to the philosophies of socialism. The Black Race in an attempt to seek out self pride and dignity turned away from assimilating into the society in which we lived and tried to adopt an African culture that we were several generations removed from.

To properly internalize a culture one must first learn that culture and then accept that culture as the truth. The Black race accepted the little information that we had about a non-specific African culture and tried to internalize it. In doing this we set ourselves apart from all other groups that had immigrated to this country. How does this influence our behavior today? How many times have you been in a supermarket or a retail store and hear a mother call out to her child, come here Shaquitha or stop that Daquan? I once asked a friend of my son what her unique name meant. Her response was I don't know. I then asked her parents what her unusual name meant. Their response was it had no specific meaning, but it sounded African.

We must understand that names are labels that we must carry with us for the rest of our lives. If you are going to make a weak attempt to connect your child to a culture that you didn't grow up in at least arm them with the meaning. I have a niece who is named Shekina Glory Brown. The Shekina Glory was the pillar of fire that held back the Egyptians while the Hebrews escaped through the parted Red Sea. Her father has explained to her many times that he gave her that name to give her strength in difficult times. Names mean things.

The disconnect that has been fostered in the Black Community has manifested it self in many different ways. The lack of success that many black youth experience in school has turned them to the streets. Feeling that they have no alternative other than the underworld, they have in large numbers embraced and justified a life of violence and crime. Look on the street corners of our major cities and you will find black drug dealers willing to sell death to their kin. Look at the statistics of black on black crime. Now the Liberal politician says that this problem can be fixed with more job availability. Let's be honest how many of these drug dealers would give up that life for an honest 9 to 5. We can continue to fool ourselves and use an enslavement that ended 135 years ago to justify the behavior of our worst. Or we can be honest and confront the fact that many elements in how we are raising our children today is having a greater affect in creating these problems. The black family is broken and needs to be fixed.

THE ANGRY BLACK WOMAN:

The ghost of Jim Crow has had many negative affects on the Black Community, but none as serious as the deplorable affect it has had on black relationships. In our rise to equality black women feel that they have been left behind, cheated out of their just do. Many black women are under the impression that the first thing a successful black man does is goes and gets his white trophy. This is the common thought among many black women. However the facts dispute this argument. The overwhelming majority of successful black men are married to black women, and they are living the American dream. Why are some black women so angry? Why are some black women having such difficult times with relationships? The answer is simple. Some black women aren't attracted to real black men. Now what is a real man? A real man is spiritual he knows his purpose. A real man is responsible and unselfish his family comes first. Most of all a real man is a protector and a leader; he offers guidance and security for his loved ones. The problem is that a lot of black women are not attracted to this kind of man. Many black women have bought into the negative stereotypes of the modern black man. He's lazy and unintelligent; he is incapable of being faithful, or being a provider. He is also angry and abusive. This is the angry black women's idea of what a man is. Yet, why so many black women have chosen to ignore the black males that have exhibited the positive characteristics of a responsible man. Many black women have ignored black men that have pursued the American dream and have taken the path of education. These black men have been labeled as white boys, geeks, wannabes, and nerds. Some black women believing that there are no real black men left have turned outside the race and demanded qualities that they neglected to demand within our own race. Instead, black women have accepted the street hustler in the belief that their love will change him into that responsible man they claim to long for. So in the process of putting on her make up, she also must display an attitude that will attract the street hustler. She becomes a tough, streetwise, no nonsense type of women that can take care of her self. Unfortunately, it works, she is successful in attracting a loser that will take advantage of her and abuse her. She works so he doesn't have to. The Liberal Feminist movement has encouraged the black female to be dominant to take the lead, to wear the pants. Yet, with the many challenges faced by Black Americans, this attitude has been counter- productive. This attitude has only attracted the street hustlers and the con men that are more than willing to let their lady work while they run the streets. When he gets her pregnant, and is unwilling or unable to fulfill the roll of father, he will abandon her and his child. After this happens a few times she will be justifiably angry and poor. That is when she will blame white women for taking all the good black men. Now this angry black woman has baggage to go along with her attitude and resentment, and this isn't attractive to any man.

This cycle needs to be stopped. We need to stop making the angry black woman. Yet where does the responsibility lie? It's obvious that women should only be involved with real men. The problem is that modern girls no longer recognize the real man, or know how to attract him. What modern girls need to do is become real women. This involves restraint, sacrifice, foresight, and submission. Now we know that submission is a dirty word to most black women, but it is a word that allows a real man to be a real man. It is a word that demands men and women to accept their proper roles in the family. If you expect a man to be a provider then let him provide. If you expect a man to be a protector then let him protect. If you expect a man to be a leader then follow him.

In order for women to do this they must possess the skills to pick a real man. Nature has given us the perfect analogy.

Take the Horn tailed swallow. The male swallow prepares himself to find a mate he cleans himself up, meticulously grooming every feather. When he finds a potential mate he does a very peculiar thing. He starts building a nest. After the nest is done, the female will inspect its location. If she thinks that the location is bad she flies off and he fails. He must now reassess his location. He must make sure that his nest is not too high, so that it is easily accessible by predatory birds, or too low were predatory mammals can attack. His location must be perfect. When he brings another potential mate to his new nest and she approves of the location. The female does something very interesting. She goes into the nest and jumps up and down vigorously, thoroughly testing the construction and quality of the nest. If the nest doesn't hold up the female swallow knows that this male swallow is unable to take care of a family.

What can black women learn from these clever birds? Do black women of today put their suitors through similar test? Lets first look at how the male swallow properly grooms himself. Women of today should take this clue and not accept street thugs with their pants hung around their knees. Instead she should look for a properly dressed male who understands the need to assimilate into society in order to succeed not those who are angry at the world and only look to intimidate.

What is the importance of location? How many blacks have found success, yet still live in poverty-stricken neighborhoods, trying to keep it real, allowing their families to be at risk from dangerous gangs and violent crime. How many young black males spend countless dollars on Spreewell rims and auto accessories, instead of investing in a safe home for their families? Black women must reject these men and instead look for the man who has the foresight to set up a home in a safe area fit to raise children, and outside the circle of poverty.

How does testing the nest compare to what black women need to do. Now we are not saying that you should go into a man's house and jump up and down and damage his hardwoods. Testing the nest is comparable to testing the character of the man. What is his quality? Is he faithful, Is he committed to the well being of his family, how does he function through hard times, can he provide a safe and nurturing home for his family. This is the hardest test. It requires that you take the time to truly get to know the man, before you marry and more important bear his children.

It's time for Black women to take responsibility for dropping the ball and not judging a man by his character, but instead jumping in bed with any man that makes her feel good. Black women have failed to understand their role in social behavior. To men a woman is the prize, and men are willing to do what ever is necessary to win a woman's favor. Black women must set high standards when choosing a mate. Only when the bar is raised, and black women force black men to rise to a higher level, will they. Black woman hold the key, and only when they stop choosing the zero over the hero will black men change their behavior for the better. Black women must understand that if a man can't follow man's law then he is incapable of following God's law, and thus is unworthy of the role of husband and father.

What effect has not following these sound biblical principles had on the Black Community? Many times I have sat back and listened to young black mothers publicly disciplining their children. I have heard less cursing on shore leave in a bar full of sailors. The complications of young, unwed motherhood have plagued our race. In today's society we are close to fatherless children becoming the norm. Today's young black males dishonor themselves and black women by having premarital sex, and having many children by different women. These children are abandoned to be raised in poverty. Abandoned by a father that if they know who he is can no more advise them about life than help them with their homework. We must wake up and put an end to this vicious cycle that we find ourselves trapped in.

Black women and young black girls need to have self respect and practice abstinence until marriage. Premarital sex is a sin and God will not be mocked. Now I know that Liberals don't believe in teaching Biblical principles in the schools, they would much rather our children learn how to use a condom. Those lessons don't address the morality of their actions. It doesn't address the hardening of the heart of young girls who use sex as bait to get the love that they lack at home.

What effect has out of wedlock births had on black children? The damage is severe. Young black girl's, lacking the love of a father; go out seeking that love in relationships. Young black males, lacking the guidance and lessons a father can give, treat young black woman like whores, and the cycle continues.

Another problem that plagues the black race is one that has been inherited from our elders. That problem is a deep-seated hatred for the white race. Hatred is a poison that will drag its participants in a hole and keep them there. Many blacks have used the racism of the past to justify their bad behavior of the present. Even our so-called Black Leaders have been guilty of this. Several years ago black parents started a riot at a Pop-Warner football game, and instead of condemning the bad behavior for what it was, our black leaders tried to justify it, in doing this loosing any credibility that they may have had.

Many blacks feel that because we as a people were treated so badly in the past that it justifies them in having racist attitudes. My father once told me "in order to hold someone in a hole, you must be willing to stay in that hole with them." In an interview with James H. Brown Sr., a 70-year-old black man who grew up under Jim Crow in the south, James was asked how he was able to grow up under such oppression, but not hate all white people. His answer was that his mother was responsible for that. He stated" my mother always told us that this oppression can't last forever, and that you must prepare yourself for when equality comes." James also said that his mother raised him with a deep love of God and that there is no blessing in hate. James' ability to throw off his hatred has allowed him to find success and assimilate into our society.

The hatred felt by many blacks for whites has been a negative force that has led to continuous failures. In many cases blacks have blamed whites for their failures, and this has kept them from addressing the real problem that they faced. I in no way mean to suggest that racism doesn't exist, but in order to move forward we as black people need to put off that hate and free ourselves from another bond.

Another problem in the black community is the ghettos or the politically correct name for them, low-income housing. This seemingly compassionate program supported by liberals is just another trap for the black community. Today's ghettos are havens for the formation of gangs, the sale of drugs, and violence.

Most people living in ghettos are being supported by the welfare system. This system that is not a program which will allow them to advance, but instead traps them and houses them in one particular area. Those living in the ghettos receive an education in poverty. An education on how to" beat the system" not realizing that it is they who are being beat out of a decent life. Even if the parents are decent and try to teach their children the proper lessons that will lead to success in life, their children are affected more with their negative surroundings.

Black children in low- income housing are challenged daily by the poisons of poverty. Drugs are prevalent in these areas, and to young minds drugs can seem like the only way out. Gang membership is either forced upon them, or offers them the unity that they lack from their family. Overall a dismal picture of life is painted for those who live in our ghettos. Different from the ghettos of the past, where two parent families worked hard to better their situation and kept their pride because they slowly accomplished goals, today's ghettos are a trap where people are given basic sustenance, housed, and forgotten until election time. Their children must watch the vicious cycle of poverty claim their friends one by one. As parents trapped in a community of drug abuse, violence, and declining morals can only pray for a better life for their children as their opportunities wither away. Black families must stay out of public housing. If this housing is so great why aren't the politicians building them moving their families in? If low-income housing is so beneficial to those with low incomes why aren't these politicians moving in their mother's who are on a fixed income so she can benefit? The answer is clear they want to keep their loved ones away from their created war zones.

THE RAP SUB-CULTURE:

The posturing and bad attitudes exhibited by today's black youth have risen to catastrophic levels. In a small city such as Syracuse, New York hardly a day has passed this summer without news of either gang violence or senseless shootings. Most who's origins are from something petty. Many of today's black youth lack the self-respect in order to be good citizens, and if they are unable to respect themselves, how can they possibly respect others? Gangs terrorize their own neighborhoods and trap decent black people in their homes in fear. While they believe that it is the white man keeping them down because this is what our so-called black leaders are telling us.

Many of the deviant behaviors and attitudes can be blamed on the sub-culture created by the rap industry. This sub-culture plays a significant role in the moral decline of our race. Through their music and visuals of music videos, today's rap stars are glorifying the underbelly of human existence. Rap stars portray themselves as masters of a ghetto-fabulous life. They create degrading fashions, behaviors, and practices that may be acceptable in the world of rap, but is repulsive on the streets of everyday America, and our youth are only to willing to emulate their musical heroes. There is nothing sadder when a young boy doesn't have the commonsense to pull up his pants and not show his underwear when attending school.

With the growing popularity of the rap culture many may mistakenly believe that these degrading fashions will become the norm. This of coarse is not true. These fashions and behaviors only act as a stereotyping tool to identify those of the lower class. The image of success and fame portrayed by even the least successful of rap artist has a strong influence on the impressionable minds of our youth who are ready and willing to emulate the most horrid behavior that they see played out before them.

Women in the rap culture are refereed to as "Bitches and Ho's", while men are revered as players and pimps. Is it not obvious to see that we continue to define ourselves down to the lowest element? Terms such as pimps and whores that once held negative meaning are now adopted as a desirable thing to be. Our values and our morals are on the steady decline heading for a crash landing.

Many negative symbols and the foulest of language and behaviors, which the rap culture glorifies in the minds of our children, become acceptable behavior. Images of gun toting thugs surrounded by loose woman to do their bidding become the desired life style to the youth of the black community. With the worldwide popularity of entertainment venues such as MTV these degrading images are what foreigners use to define what a black American is.

I remember when I was stationed in Okinawa, Japan and the only American television station available was Armed Force Network. I was insulted because the only images of black Americans were frequent news reports of Los Angles gang violence and television shows showing blacks in poverty. I remember when I met my mother-in-law to be. My behavior and demeanor surprised her because the only images that she had to educate herself about black Americans were degrading images of violence, broadcast via the biased mass media. These images have more of an effect than we can imagine.

While I was stationed in Japan my wife worked in a Japanese restaurant. Her co-worker, a Japanese woman we called Mama Jo Anne, asked me to come to her house to meet her daughter. She explained that her daughter was visiting from the mainland and that she had a very negative view of black Americans. She stated that I was different from the stereotypes that her daughter feared, and she wanted her daughter to see that all black men weren't violent. I saw this invitation as an honor and accepted. To my disappointment her daughter refused to stay in the same room with me. I saw fear in her eyes and her body shaking with fear. Where did this foreign girl, who had never met a black man, develop this fear? It couldn't have been from experience. It came from the one sided presentation she received from the American media. This powerful tool has spread the underbelly of urban culture and represented it as black culture.

Even the suburbs and rural America are no longer safe from the damaging influences of gangster rap. White suburbia teens now imitate the deviant fashions and behaviors that they see on MTV and through Hollywood's movies. They have even been given a name of their own, wiggers. For those of you, who can't figure that one out, white niggers.

Many Rap stars when confronted with the negative effect that their music has on black youth fall back on the age old liberal response that they are just portraying how things are, they are a mirror on society. A mirror only reflects what is; the sub-culture of rap is creating deviance and glorifying that which we should be ashamed of. All of these artist need to take a look in the mirror and ask themselves is what I'm doing benefiting my community, my race, my country?

One effect of this sub-culture that caught me by surprise is the effect that it has on black foreigners. Refugees from countries such as Sudan that once excelled and exhibited integrity and dignity are now assimilating into urban culture. Their once respectful demeanor has been replaced with the coarse rude attitudes exhibited by many black American youth.

We as black people need to stop defining black behavior as deviant behavior. We need to stop identifying ourselves with sinful disgusting behavior. We must stop thinking that any behavior labeled as black must be opposite to what is thought of as white. When a black child in school achieves good grades we must stop labeling their behavior as acting white, and when a black person speaks the English language with articulation we must stop thinking that "he is talking white". What will we allow the identifying factors of black America to be? Will we allow pants bagging, gun toting, women abusing, foulmouthed thugs to be the internationally accepted image of what black is, or will the silent majority of the black community finally rise up and show the world that we are a decent moral people.

In years past our identifier was the church .The church is where our moral reference was formed. With the acceptance of liberalism by the black community comes the fragmentation of a moral reference. Our Leadership has justified bad behavior and tried to use civil rights to excuse the shortcomings of some blacks. They have labeled us as ignorant and incompetent and in constant need of government assistance. They have identified us with poverty and we now accept that this is the status of a black American, that we are incapable of morality because of discrimination in the past. After years of hearing from the liberals and our own black leadership that we are less, we as a people finally believe it.

The message of conservatism has been uplifting. Black people are just as capable as our white counterparts, that we need no government assistance, just an equal playing field in which the hunt for success takes place. The plans that Conservatives present to the black community is one that will fix long term problems not just pacify us. Yet, the black community has rejected this message, and we have battled for the scraps that our liberal representation was willing to brush off the table for us. Our black leaders have betrayed us by not weaning us off the government nipple fearing the dissolution of their status of leaders. Groups like the NAACP have been unwilling to even listen and engage conservatives and just proclaim them to be racist. Just as any black person that dare think that there may be a better way to solve our problems is labeled an Uncle Tom or a lap dog for the republicans.

It is time that we as black people take our rightful place as citizens of this country. We must look for different ways to resolve the issues that confront us. We have tried the liberal/socialist path since the late 1960's, and things have gotten worse. The only way we can progress is to stop looking to the government to supply our daily needs. We must stop looking to government for programs such as daycare for our children, welfare, and healthcare. This is not the purpose of government. We must trust in our own abilities, it is truly liberating to know that your destiny lies in your hands and not the passage of another government program.

Chapter 9

Why Is Conservatism Right for the Black Community?

When we sat down and looked at this work, we saw that something was missing.

Although we had discussed many points where we showed that the conservatives through history had done more for the black race, we felt we needed to give a clear presentation of what conservatism is and why it's right for the black race. In this last chapter we will do a point by point comparison of Conservatism vs. Liberalism and then discuss why conservatism is better for the black race.

POVERTY:

Not only in our society, but also in every known society there have always been the rich and the poor. The Liberals plan to fight poverty is the creation of more social programs. The plan that liberalism offers is socialism. At first glance this seems to be the most compassionate plan, but socialism attempts to put a band-aid on the ulcer of poverty. This approach that has been tried since the early 1960's has created a larger lower class, and has systematically brought about an increased rate of social problems. The traps that go along with a system that doesn't encourage it participants to seek constant improvement in their lives have ensnared many in the black race. Liberalism seeks to give a fish to the masses so that they can eat today. This approach offers no self-reliant message and depends on those who are innovative and strive to improve to provide for those who are not. To take away from those who earn, to support those who do not. Karl Marx's Ideal utopia was true communism, a world where all is shared equally. The problem with his theory is it has no producers. All Communist and Socialist Governments have failed. Where there is no reward for innovation, innovation will not exist.

Conservatism offers a plan of self-reliance and capitalism. Capitalism is what has set this country apart from all others and made it great. Capitalism rewards the creativity and the innovation of its participants. This is why the United States leads the world in invention and technology. Conservatism mirrors the rugged determination of our founding fathers and depends only on the driving force of the spirit of those who seek to better their lives. Conservatism believes in teaching you to fish so that you can eat every day. It inspires you to find better ways to fish. The conservative approach to poverty looks not to sustain the poor, but to eradicate poverty. Conservatives don't seek to make the poor comfortable in poverty; they seek to help the poor out of poverty.

The Black community, through many trials and challenges, has survived. Since the 1960's we have staked our advancement on the philosophies and policies of liberalism. Are we satisfied with where it has gotten us? I believe in the creativity and the innovation of the black race, and only by freeing ourselves and depending only on ourselves, not the government, to better our situation will we realize the great accomplishments that we as a people have to offer. I call on the spirit of those in Hopson City, in Allensworth, and in Rosewood to return to the whole of the black race your spirit of innovation and self-reliance, and to ignite us to reach our potential.

Under the policies of Ronald Regan, more blacks advanced from the lower class to the middle class than any other time in our history. Throughout history blacks have achieved more when the government gave less. We as a people need to throw off the ghost of Jim Crow and prepare ourselves for success. I believe that the road of conservatism will lead us there.

EDUCATION:

Education is an issue that we as Americans should put as the number one priority. State governments struggle to finance school budgets, while votes for their pay increase pass in secret late hour sessions. Although money seems to be the major problem in our schools it's not. The problems that we face in schools can't be fixed by throwing more money at them. The problem that no one wants to speak of is that we have many children who don't want to learn. A child who has the desire to learn is easy to teach. It is as natural as feeding a newborn. The problems that we face in society have overflowed into our public schools creating children with no understanding of the value of a good education. Teachers are challenged in their classrooms to use unavailable time to address behavioral issues, while trying to educate those children who truly desire an education. The Conservative answer to these problems differs from the Liberal answer.

The Liberals choose to throw good money at bad. They continue to throw more funding at school programs that are not working. Schools where large percentages of the students are unable to pass basic reading and math test, and some teachers, who can't pass that same test, continue to receive funding. Children in these schools suffer while year after year no significant changes are made. Teachers unions protect teachers, who are not blessed with the gift of teaching, because they have tenure.

Conservatives, on the other hand, support school vouchers and teacher competency testing. Schools where children are trapped in violence and poor standards would be forced to raise the standard or be closed. If they can't properly educate our children should they remain open? Parents would be given the funds to send their children to schools that have proven that they can do the job. Our children would receive the foundational teaching that would enable them to succeed. Teachers would have to pass state test proving that they have the knowledge to teach our children properly.

The Conservative plan is better for the black race. Many inner city black youth lay trapped in non-performing schools and they are not being taught the foundational lessons needed. These children are passed along without the proper educational structure to understand the lessons of the higher grades. These children are failures in the waiting. In high school when they should be learning trigonometry and calculus, they struggle with the basic math they should have learned earlier. The voucher system puts the choice in the parent's hands. If your child's school is unable to maintain acceptable standards you have the option to move them to a school that has proven their worth.

TAXES:

Taxes should be an issue that we all agree on. We should agree that we pay too much. The Liberal and Conservative are on different sides of the fence when it comes to basic philosophies pertaining to taxes.

Liberals believe in raising taxes. They believe the only way to fill the government coffers is to fleece its people. Liberals believe that it is necessary to raise taxes to pay for the multitude of social programs that they seek to maintain. The only thing that these social programs are successful in doing is creating the need for more money and new social programs to fix the problems created by the earlier programs.

By raising the taxes on individuals and businesses the liberals send the economy in a downward spiral. The consumer (you and me) having to pay higher taxes have less money to spend. Having less money to spend we purchase less; businesses having to pay higher taxes and not selling as much (remember you and I are spending less) makes less money. Selling less the retailer orders less from the manufacturer. I find it necessary to explain the purpose of business is to make money. Businesses, making less money, cut their expenses, in order to hold their profit margin; manufactures having less orders lay-off employees. The largest expense to a business is their employees. In order to hold their profit margin the retailer lays-off employees. With fewer people working fewer people are paying taxes. The government takes in less in taxes.

This scenario affects the individual, the manufacturers, and the retailers. Multiply this scenario by millions. All participants in our economy are affected negatively. While the liberals continue to raise taxes and over spend when it comes to the national budget, and our society suffers from the problems created by a socialist philosophy.

Conservatives believe in cutting taxes. Conservatives believe that no one can better decide where to spend your money than you.

In cutting taxes on the individual and businesses, the individual (you and me) has more money to spend. As proven by the 2001-2002 Bush tax cuts, when people are given their money back they spend it. The month after the tax rebate checks were received was a record month for Wal-Mart. The manufacture making more money in sales and having to pay less in business taxes invest its earnings in more manpower and more orders from the manufactures of goods. The manufacturer having more orders needs more employees to fill these orders. With more people working and thus more people paying taxes, the government takes in more in taxes.

Another area of taxes where the two philosophies differ is the Estate Tax better known as the Death Tax. The current rate of the Estate Tax is from 45%-55%. What does this mean for you and me? That after years of struggling and working hard to buy a home and build something to leave to our children, that when we are called home to glory, our children will have to pay a 45%-55% tax on the value of what ever we are able to leave them. Most people think that this tax only applies to the rich. You are wrong.

The Liberals have fought off many attempts to lower and to eliminate the Estate tax by the Conservatives. They, the Liberals, claim that their not going to lower any taxes on the rich. This tax affects us all.

These are but a few points about taxes. It is clear to see that the conservative philosophy towards taxes is beneficial to the black race. With the increase of black millionaires through business, sports, and the entertainment fields, we should be able to pass on the wealth that we have acquired. Instead of our children having to give 45%-55% of what we leave for them to the government.

Pertaining to our everyday taxes, is it not better to keep more of our money? Shouldn't we decide where we spend our money, whether to spend it, save it, or invest it?

The social programs that the liberals claim to raise taxes to pay for don't work. They only create more and more expensive problems to fix. We as Black people need to stop looking for the next social program to cure our ills. They only create more problems for us.

SOCIAL SECURITY:

President George W. Bush has proposed changing social security. This program has been in place to offer a safety net to those who are negligent or unable to save for retirement. Yet since the creation of this program the cost of living has increased to a point that no one could possible live on social security benefits alone. The changes proposed by this Republican administration would allow a small portion of the social security tax, which are presently being collected, to be invested into the stock market. Over the years long term investments in the stock market have shown substantial gains and have consistently offered a higher rate of return then the present social security.

How would this new program benefit the black community? It is a well-known fact that Black Americans, because of illness such as hypertension, and diabetes have a lower life expectancy than the national average. Under the new social security plan, money set aside in investment funds can be willed to a participant's family or friends. Different from the current situation that we find ourselves, when someone dies before retirement age the monies collected over a lifetime return to the general fund, unless you have children still in school. Under the new program we would be able to pass on the money that we have worked a lifetime for on to our families.

The Republican plan for social security would also be beneficial because it would give a higher rate of return than the current system, by the way that is at risk to go bankrupt.

Many older Black Americans are dependent on social security for their retirement. If we don't support the political philosophy that is willing to fix this problem these monies my not be there for us when our retirement time comes.

When President Franklin D. Roosevelt created social security we had a ratio of 16 workers to every social security recipient. At present time the ratio is at 3.3 workers to every 1 recipient. With every improving technology and medical research people are living longer. Thus we need to find a fix for this program before it goes bust. The Liberals answer is to just do nothing. During the years of the Clinton administration, and during the 2000 presidential election, social security was a major issue. We all can remember Vice-Presidents Al Gore's famous *lock box* approach to fixing social security. Yet now that they, the liberals, are out of power there is no longer a need to fix this desperate power. One is left wondering about their true motives.

MINIMUM WAGE:

On the surface this seems to be an issue that is very clear. Of course the minimum wage should be raised so that everyone can afford a better living. Right! The Liberals have pushed to raise the minimum wage and have claimed to do this in the interest of the poor. Conservatives have opposed any raise in the minimum wage claiming that raising the minimum wage would cost jobs.

First off, let's take an honest look at basic employment. How many adult workers have started working a new job and have been started at minimum wage and still find themselves there six months later. If this is the case, you need to look for another job. If you work for an employer who after six month hasn't given you a raise, he's cheap and you will be none the worse going to Mc Donald's or Burger King, who by the way currently start their employees out at about $6.25 per hour.

Raising the minimum wage will cost jobs. Most employees that you find working for minimum wage are high school students. This is usually the first venture into the work place and they are gaining valuable work experience along with a humble salary. Raising the minimum wage will make it so that small businesses are unable to afford to hire that extra summer help. City budgets, which are already stretched to their limits, won't be able to hire as many high school students to work for Parks and Recs.

The plans that Liberals support are meant to give very little assistance while placing the entire burden on businesses. That results in layoffs and less summer jobs.

The Conservative plan is realistic and meant to create permanent advancement.

Instead of looking for the government to raise your salary go get training in a skill that will pay you a higher wage. The current federal minimum wage is $ 5.15, if you work a standard 40-hour week you would earn $ 10,712 per year gross. Raising the minimum wage to $6.00 per hour would raise your yearly earnings to $12, 480, a gain of $1,768 per year. This small amount is not going to change anyone's life; it leaves you struggling in poverty.

A licensed practitioner nurse is a job that one can train for in eight months. It is not the easiest training to complete and will take hard work and sacrifice, but the starting pay is on average about $ 12.50 per hour. You would earn $26,000 per year with this training. Most nurses are members of a national union, which negotiates raises. Taking the situation into your own hands is going to benefit you more than relying on the crumbs the federal government can push off the table for you.

The black community needs to stop waiting for the government to force businesses to pay more money than some jobs are worth. We need to take our own destiny in our own hands and educate ourselves in jobs and trades in which we can expect a decent wage. We need to desire more than the minimal existence. The Conservative plan doesn't seek to increase your comfort with poverty. It understands that the human spirit desires more. We live in a competitive economy, we as black people need to prepare ourselves to compete and stop sitting on the sidelines waiting for the crumbs that the victor is willing to give us. We as a people have much more than that to offer.

TORT REFORM:

Tort Reform is an issue that most people feel doesn't relate to them. It has also been one of the most misunderstood political issues.

Tort is defined as: damage, injury, or wrongful act done willfully, negligently, or in circumstances involving strict liability, but not involving breach of contract, for which a civil suit can be brought. The Liberals stance has been anti-tort reform, because they claim that tort reform will take away an individuals right to sue to compensate for damages. This is not accurate representation of what tort reform hopes to accomplish. Tort reform seeks to eliminate abuses off our legal system, a system that has been bogged down by frivolous lawsuits and exorbitant pay outs on judgments, judgments like the well-known Mc Donald's $10,000,000 coffee case. In this case a women won a judgement against Mc Donald's Corporation because as she drove off from the drive through she spilled her coffee on her lap, and claimed to get second and third degree burns, she stated she didn't realize the coffee was hot. Now let's assume that Mc Donald's is guilty of negligent overheating. How can one justify a judgement of $10,000,000? This obvious sympathetic judgement represents how torts have gotten out of control. With today's hostile environment towards corporation, they are easy targets for ambulance chasing, hospital lobby stalking, over billing parasite lawyers.

Now juries my not have the foresight to see the damage that these excessive judgements have on not only the Corporation, but on the average consumer as well.

Excessive judgements have caused insurance companies to recoup their losses by raising the rates on all consumers. According to the 1995 Rand study *The Cost of Excess Medical Claims for Automobile Personal Injuries.* "Excess consumption of health care in the auto arena in response to Tort liability incentives accounted for about $4,000,000,000 in 1993. The Rand study also estimates that non-economic and other losses resulting from excessive claiming behavior cost insures another $9 -$13,000,000,000 annually ". (Saxton 8)

The Conservatives have been Pro-Tort reform. The Conservatives have lobbied to put limits to actual damages and halting the excessive judgements for punitive damages that we have seen a steep rise in the last twenty years. With the pattern of excessive judgements the system has experienced more fraudulent cases by people looking for lottery size payoffs for obviously non-negligent acts by companies. Individuals believing that it's only the insurance companies' money, I'm not hurting anyone, but we all pay the price for these excessive judgements by paying higher premiums for our insurance, such as auto- insurance and health insurance.

How does all this affect the black community? Successful Tort reform would benefit the black community by first lowering the cost of auto insurance premiums. The Rand study estimated that with Tort reform low-income driver could expect a 45 percent reduction in premiums compared to a 28 percent nationwide reduction for premiums. (Saxton 6)

Secondly, successful Tort reform would affect the accessibility to health care for those of lower income. Healthcare costs have skyrocketed because doctors have to pay unbelievably high premiums for malpractice insurance. These costs are passed on to the consumer and limit access to healthcare by lower income patients. Reform is likely to have a significant impact in medical malpractice cases. Cases where clear negligence exists will likely be settled more quickly, clearing the courts of the frivolous and the fraudulent give more time to the legitimate cases that deserve to be heard.

The Conservatives plan of positive Tort reform is clearly the plan that is more advantageous to the black community. By lowering premiums of auto insurance and making healthcare more accessible to the masses this will allow the minority community to keep more of their workable income to spend on more vital living expenses.

ABORTION:

Abortion is one of the most intense issues on the modern day political landscape. For many in our society, this is a single issue voting decision-maker. An abortion is the termination of a pregnancy before its full term by a variety of methods. The two major political parties couldn't be farther apart on where they stand on this issue

Liberals support abortion and a woman's right to privacy with her body. Liberals believe that since a fetus is inside a woman's body, and totally dependent on that woman for sustaining its life, that she should have total control for the outcome of its life. A fetus has no value. It is just a useless mass of flesh, sort of like your tonsils. Strangely enough liberals also don't think that performing an abortion on a minor is any of the parents business. They feel that it is detrimental to inform the parents of their daughter's decision to end a life. Liberals don't feel that the parents should have the right to council their child on this very serious decision; she can be counseled better at school or maybe at Planned Parenthood. Also, Liberals don't take the fathers into consideration; he doesn't even exist in the mind of those on the left. Liberals take abortion a step further with their support of partial birth abortion. This procedure, which is performed in the third trimester of a pregnancy, is dangerous to the mother and of course the baby and some babies have experienced birth during this procedure just to have that life snuffed out.

Conservatives, on the other hand, oppose abortion. For Conservatives, abortion is the extinguishing of a life, killing of a baby, or just plain murder.

Abortion is shunned by every civilized religion in the world. Having children is encouraged" *be fruitful and multiply",* but also be responsible parents. It is the parent's duty to take care of their child. If the child was unplanned, or the parents are unable to care for it, it's their duty and responsibility to see that a strong two parent family adopts their child and provides the household that will offer a positive upbringing. This is just decent behavior. Behavior that we were all raised with, but we choose to ignore for our convenience. All life is precious, but innocent life is special. Conservatives know that a woman can't have a baby by herself, what about the desires of the father? Since he played a part in this creation shouldn't he have some say in this decision?

Conservatives also support the rights of parents to oversee every aspect of their child's upbringing, and the thought of schools letting a minor have an operation without the consent of the parents is criminal.

As for the black community, most blacks have this issue right. The overwhelming majority of blacks don't support abortion. It goes against the teachings of the church, and the extended black family culture. Most blacks know that abortion is birth control for the upper middle class blacks and middle class whites. Contrary to what you may have heard, middle and lower class blacks keep their babies. The question we have for the black community is, why are you supporting the politician that are using the poor black community as an excuse to give the upper class their birth control? Most of the modern black leaders call themselves men of God. Where is the outrage over all the dead babies?

What do they think will happen if they call out their liberal friends on the lies about abortion in the black community, no more government handouts? Sad to think, that we would let a baby die for a welfare check. Isn't our integrity worth more than that?

Further more abortion is just not something the black community needs to support. We of all people shouldn't accept any attempt to rip families apart, or any attempt to weaken the position of the role of the black father. Like the welfare system abortion devalues the role of fatherhood to the point of irrelevance. On the contrary black men need to stand up and take responsibility for their families. Our young black males don't need anything else to aid in their irresponsibility.

Abortion is too easy utilized after an unexpected pregnancy. A young black male doesn't have to rise up and take responsibility, if his girlfriend would just kill his problem. Instead of abortion, black men shouldn't dishonor themselves by having meaningless sex with several women. Black parents should learn to sacrifice for their child. If the child was unexpected, and you are unable to rise to the challenges of child rearing, show the child the ultimate act of love. Put the child up for adoption and let him live. You never know he could be the next Martin or Malcolm.

GUN CONTROL:

This is another issue that you might think it's clear to see which view is better. With the steady rise in the crime rate over the last forty years, one might think that the answer is to get rid of the guns. Get rid of the guns and the crime will stop. Anti-gun lobbyist point to countries like Japan, whose strict gun laws all but take full credit for their low crime rates. When in reality it is more an issue of culture.

The Liberals believe that the only way to impact the ever-increasing crime rate is to remove the guns from the hands of its citizens. They believe that laws that require background checks and waiting periods to legally buy a gun will keep guns out of the hands of criminals. Unfortunately this is not true. Most guns used to commit a violent crime have been stolen or illegally purchased. By passing more and more restrictive laws on gun control we only keep guns out of the hands of honest citizens.

During his term as president, President Bill Clinton proposed suspending the need for a search warrant so that the police could round up all the illegal guns in a Detroit housing project. This follows a philosophical pattern of liberalism to slowly take away the rights guaranteed to us by the Constitution. The projects are not the only place where gun violence happens. If it was necessary to suspend civil rights in a Detroit project, why not suspend that right nationally.

Oddly enough that was not the first time that black citizens were singled out concerning gun control. The original idea of gun control was conceived in order to keep blacks from owning any weapons with which they could protect themselves. Historical records provide compelling evidence that racism underlies gun control laws. Since their inception gun control laws openly stated that their goal was to keep guns out of the hands of Blacks and Hispanics.

Racist arms laws predate the establishment of the United States. In 1751, the French Black Code required Louisiana colonist to stop any blacks, and if necessary, beat "any black carrying any potential weapon" such as a cane. If the Black was on horseback the colonist was authorized to "shoot to kill". (Cramer 1)

In Maryland during colonial times the government went as far as to restricting blacks from owning dogs without a proper license fearing that blacks may use dogs as weapons to protect themselves. The government authorized any white citizen to kill any unlicensed dog owned by a free black. Mississippi took things a step further; they outlawed any ownership of a dog by a free black. The restriction on black slaves goes way back, but restrictions on gun ownership of free blacks predates it.

Other states had laws that were just as blatantly racist. North Carolina asserted in an 1840 statue that stated:

That if any free Negro, mulatto, or free person of color, shall wear or carry about his or her person, or keep in his or her house, any shot gun, musket, rifle, pistol, sword, dagger, or bowie-knife, unless he or she shall have obtained a license therefor from the Court of Pleas and Quarter Sessions of his or her county, within one year preceding the wearing, keeping or carrying therefor, he or she shall be guilty of a misdemeanor, and may be indicted therefor. (Cramer 2)

Restrictive gun laws didn't end with the emancipation. During the Reconstruction Era, Black Codes were passed in order to restrict the ownership of weapons that blacks could use with which to protect themselves. The Knight Riders of the Ku Klux Klan found it difficult to terrorize freed blacks that were returning fire.

Conservatives are against restrictive gun control laws; we are guaranteed the right to bear arms under the Second Amendment of the Constitution. If we would enforce the current laws we have on the books then we might have a chance to affect gun violence.

The Black Community shouldn't support any laws that try to restrict or remove any rights that are guaranteed to us. Many people struggled and died to give us such freedoms. Will we so easily give them away?

SUMMARY:

In this chapter we choose several different issues that should be used in order for people to make their voting decision. Since the 1960's the black race has supported the Democratic Party. All the while the democrats have supported an agenda that has not been in our best interest. The Democrats have promised social programs in order to secure the black race as a constant voting block, and we have given it to them. 90% of blacks vote for the democratic candidates. How could we have been so fooled?

The Presidential election of 1964 is where the big turn around happened. Congressman Barry Goldwater was the Republicans candidate for President. He was openly anti-civil rights. Dr Martin Luther King Jr. went to the Republican National committee and asked for them to remove their support from Congressman Goldwater. Needless to say they didn't. At that time Dr. King delivered the black vote to the Democrats.

We can't disagree with that decision at that time, but we often wonder if Dr. King was alive today, and seeing the disarray that plagues the black race. Where would he deliver the black vote? Which political party better represents the values and morals dear to the black race? Would Dr. King support a political philosophy that looks to remove the one stabilizing force in the black community, God?

As more and more blacks are educating themselves about politics we are starting to realize that the Republican Party more represents the direction that we are traveling. We are refusing to be sheep lead to the slaughter by organizations like the NAACP, whose interests are more financial than moral. The NAACP has answered only to the Democratic Party and has paid no attention to where it has led us. They have failed in their stewardship of the black race. They have toted the Democratic Party line and not even investigated what Conservatism had to offer the black race.

Fear not, there is a growing movement of Black Americans towards the Conservative Party. Black people who desire to be true to their roots and follow the party that is on the side of God and righteousness. The party that lives family values and doesn't' just give it lip service during election time. Black Conservatives led by such leaders as Clarence Thomas, Alan Keyes, J.C. Watts, and Condolezza Rice. This movement is quietly growing, and one day will reshape the course of American politics.

CHAPTER 10

WHERE DO WE GO FROM HERE?

So, now that the truth has been exposed, where do we go from here? It is one thing to know the truth, but it takes real courage and conviction to be able to accept it and change our direction. It would be easier to go along with the status quo, and change nothing, but what will become of us, as a race, if we continue on our current path. I fear destruction.

I was recently reading an issue of Ebony magazine, and as they do every year around this time they highlighted the top 100 Black High School Seniors. As I read through this impressive article I felt encouraged looking at the level of commitment of these young Americans at the beginning of their journey. Hopefully in this list I was reading about some of tomorrows great American leaders. Being young in America presents many barriers to success. Add being black to the equation, and you add a whole new set of barriers to conquer. Yet these barriers must be conquered. We must put out the message that no matter what barriers are put in our path that we as a people will overcome.

The message that has been put out by the current black leadership is one that has sought to fight the battle from the position of a victim, relying on the good will and guilty feelings of past acts by those in power. This is where we need to change our strategy. The conservative message recognizes not only the ability of Black Americans, but asks them to join those traveling towards success, while the liberal message seeks to compensate for the past. We need to fight this fight from the position of an equal, embracing this country as our own and ready to take part in making it a better place for all races, and not just focused on ourselves.

In this chapter we will cover important changes in direction and attitudes that need to occur within the black community. Changes that will convert us from a victim looking for a handout, to the equally talented Americans we are. It is time that we take our rightful place in the history of the America we helped build.

ASSIMILATE TO SUCCESS:

The black community has always viewed themselves as a separate entity inside a nation, similar to the plight of the Native Americans. This country has much to offer, yet in order for us to take advantage of such success we must become part of the whole. We must stop viewing ourselves as a subculture oppressed by our captures. We must believe that by following the proven path of education that we can obtain equality. The black race has held on to an African culture that has set us outside the main culture of this country. Unlike other races that have immigrated to this land, we seek to segregate ourselves from the mainstream. Immigrants to this country see education as the equalizer it is.

After the death of Dr. Martin Luther King Jr., the black race struggled to look for its identity. Unfortunately the self-imposed black leaders of the time took us down the path of the victim. They viewed what the American Government had done for the Native Americans as positive and tried to secure for the black race similar compensation. This policy of seeking compensation for past acts backfired. Where blacks of the pre-civil rights era worked hard and recognized that only through education would we stand a chance at success in this country; the post-civil rights movement created many blacks standing in line waiting for compensation for the wrongs that were done. We as a people chose to follow the RAINBOW to the promised pot of gold, yet what we found at the end was empty promises and a loss of the hunger to educate our children and ourselves. We found ourselves fighting for the scraps that the government brushed off the table.

Not unlike the Native American the blacks that accepted and depended on the compensation of welfare have again found themselves stuck in the state of a second class citizen, depending on the government for their daily bread. This system that has crippled a large percentage of those who partake of it can only promise poverty and the many ills that accompany it. Today's Black Americans must reject this weak form of compensation and position themselves to claim their rightful place as citizens of the United States of America. We must proudly stand on our own and take responsibility for when we fly or fall. When you truly have the equal right to succeed, with that comes the equal right to fail. The message from our leaders must change. Instead of fighting for programs that label use as less, work within the black communities to ensure that we are equally qualified to take advantage of the opportunities that are available. The fight that was led by Dr. Martin Luther King didn't seek to create an advantage or special treatment for blacks. He looked to receive equal rights and equal treatment under the law for blacks.

The Black Americans that have looked to work within this society and have not looked for an advantage are those who have found success. Those who have stepped out of the line waiting on the government to deliver the success that only an individual can achieve those who have trusted in their own abilities and looked to do it on their own. We have found success.

Blacks of today seek to separate themselves from the society that we live in. Today's black youth's have created a subculture outside the world of success. They look to redefine what is considered the norms within the mainstream of society. These practices may find success for those in the world of entertainment, but at a heavy price for the average everyday Black American youth. The average Black American youth is left lacking the skills, professionally and socially, needed to be successful.

Our civil rights leaders of the past fought for the right to fully interact within this society, the right to eat at the same restaurants, the right to drink from the same faucets, the right to live among White Americans. Today's Black Americans seek to segregate themselves. At many colleges Blacks seek all black dorms and all black clubs. When will we as a people start to heal and view ourselves as Americans instead of African Americans?

The Constitution of the United States, specifically the Bill of Rights was set up to guarantee the rights of all Americans. Because of slavery, bad judges, and evil men blacks were not viewed as human beings. Because of the success of the civil rights movement, we as blacks need to embrace this document and look to it to ensure our rights. We must put away the feelings that the Constitution is not for us. Instead we need to use it as a tool for our advancement. The Founding Fathers of this great nation in their great wisdom realized the evils of slavery, but they also realized that change takes time. In the Constitution they planted the seeds that would in the future bring about the end of slavery. Instead of viewing the Constitution as the document that enslaved us we need to change our prospective, and realize that it was those very laws that brought about our freedom.

TRUE POVERTY PREVENTION:

The black race has always been identified with poverty. Our current black leaders have used this fact in order to lobby the government for programs designed to rescue an entire race from the grips of poverty. The result has been the direct opposite. Our black leadership in condemning our capitalistic system has caused many blacks to seek success outside the accepted pathway. Too many black youth look to succeed through athletics or entertainment. The picture of black success in America has changed from the operating rooms and courtrooms to a lucrative sports contract or a record deal. While some are lucky enough to achieve the highest level in the fields of entertainment and sports most are left unprepared for success once the dream of stardom is shattered by reality.

We as a people must retrain ourselves to put the dream of stardom in its proper prospective. It is a very small percentage of people that find success through the entertainment and sports fields, yet a large percentage of black youths spend countless hours preparing for a life of fame. We must redirect these energies back to the classroom.

One of the predominant arguments for affirmative action was that black children needed to see blacks in certain jobs so that they could visualize themselves there. What is it that black children see today? Their picture of success is Michael Jordan, Ice Cube, 50-Cent etc… But in reality how many of our children will be able to achieve that level of success in these fields? Not that a child should be discouraged from living their dreams, but there must be an ounce of reality served along with that dream. Today's black children are unable to visualize success in the classroom, so they are unwilling to make the sacrifices necessary to be successful. An aspiring NBA hopeful will spend countless hours working on his free throws, his dribbling, and his three point shot, but will spend limited time studying math and science because they can't visualize themselves getting an A in the classroom.

When reality sets in and many of our children are left unprepared for success outside the life of fame and fortune they are damned to a life of poverty.

So what are we to do? The temptations of fame and fortune are hard for anyone to resist. How do we get the message across that one must prepare themselves for success? Part of the answer lies in the message that we send out about the possibilities and opportunities that are available. The message that our current black leaders deliver is that white America won't let blacks succeed, that because of impoverished conditions black children are disadvantaged and not as capable. This was not the message delivered to us by the late Dr. Martin Luther King Jr. He spoke of equal opportunity and never believed that blacks lacked abilities. Whether our current black leadership truly believes we are incapable or not this has been the result of the message they carry. Many blacks believe that they will not even be given a chance. So we are putting all our eggs in one basket, and following a path that only a small percentage of us will find success on.

Another area where we as a race must change our prospective is on self-reliance. Since the death of Dr. King and the drastic change in strategy concerning civil rights, blacks have looked to the government for their success. We need to understand that all the government can deliver is to keep us at the level of poverty. We as a people must accept the responsibility for our situation. When we do this we are free to make the needed changes. We must educate ourselves and arm ourselves with the tools in order to succeed. There will still be barriers to break through; anything worth having always comes with sacrifice and hard work. If we stop looking to the government and blaming it for or condition we can start to do the work needed to fix it. The government was never able to deliver us from poverty. This is something that only we can do. We have the power.

We in the black community need to start supporting black businesses. This seems like a no brainer, but it is something that is not happening. Look throughout the black communities you find a large percentage of the businesses owned by non-blacks, and when a black business owner is present blacks will travel miles outside their community to shop elsewhere. This is a major difference between blacks and other ethnic groups that have immigrated to this country. My father once told me that "the black community is like a bucket full of black crabs, when one tries to crawl out the others grab on to hold him back." We need to change our attitude on success. When a black person reaches success many within the black community look to exile them, they state that this person is no longer black, and can no longer understand our plight. Those blacks that have achieved success need to be used as a resource of knowledge for the rest of the black community. It only makes sense that if you seek to bake a cake then goes to a baker that has successfully done so. We must start to embrace those in the black community that have risen out of the depths of poverty and allow them to guide us.

We need to take a new approach to poverty prevention for decades after the civil rights movement we as a people have looked to the government to deliver us from poverty, when in truth we possess the escape within ourselves. There is no program that the government can pass that will give us the tools needed to advance our fiscal situation. Now many will say that this is unfair and even racist, quite the contrary. I look at what the black community was able to achieve under the restrictions of Jim Crow and unequal rights and believe that we are capable of so much more under the current state of equality. I think that if we get back to the road that Dr. Martin Luther King Jr. traveled that we and only we can fix the problems within our communities that is the true barrier to our success.

REBUILD THE TRADITIONAL FAMILY:

This is probably the most important element to fixing the problems within the black community. Slavery ripped the black family apart and it took years to rebuild it. Yet up until the late 1960's and early 1970's the black traditional family experienced resurgence. The introduction of drugs into our communities led us down a path of crime and immorality.

The adoption of the welfare system gave blacks the so- called compensation for the years of injustice that we suffered, or did it? Those who receive these benefits are punished for trying to keep the traditional family intact. Fathers are not allowed to live in the home. Many black men both unskilled and unable to secure a reasonable wage to support their families or those just too lazy to look have left it to the government to raise their children. Black children void of the positive male role model have turned to immorality because they are taught no better.

One of the true causalities of this situation has been the black female. Young girls raised without the love of a strong father venture out at an early age looking for the love they lacked from daddy. What they find is young men who have not been instructed on the role and responsibility father and husband and are unable to step up to the plate. This cycle has continued and deteriorated since the early 1970's. How do we fix such an enormous problem? We must look to what we allow to guide us. The answers to our problems are simple, we as a people must be willing to accept them and implement them. The answer is the family. Our children need to be raised in supportive and loving two-parent homes. Black men need to stop having several children by several different women. Black women need to raise their standards and demand more of those who come to court. This problem is cyclical, when dad doesn't stay home to raise his boys and girls he leaves them lacking relationship skills that they need in order to interact in a healthy relationship. Young men now think it is acceptable to impregnate a woman and walk away. Young black girls are no longer surprised to find themselves alone raising several different men's children. We have reached the point where we don't expect much more than this.

Black men we must be willing to accept the responsibilities of heading a household and deserving of the respect we demand from women. We must understand that our life's purpose is to raise smart, healthy, and honest citizens. Child rearing is filled with sacrifice. Sacrifice that many black men are unwilling to make. I can't imagine where I would be had I not had a strong father who constantly taught me and guided me towards manhood. Black men wake up and stop leaving our children to be raised by the government we claim to be so unfair. We as black men need to understand that the problems start with us, and in us lies the answer. We are the one's that need to get back on the right track. If we do this black women will gladly follow.

Black women hold up a high standard. I have listened to so many black women state that there are no good men out there. You need to wait instead of settling. Black women need to wait for the man who is ready and excited about starting a family; those men who are ready to give their life in their family's defense. Those men like my father that even though the marriage didn't work, he would never abandon his children. Black women need to return to old fashion traditions of waiting until marriage before having sex.

The feminist revolution told women that they didn't need men. The sexual revolution told you that you could be as sexually liberated as men. Are you happy with what you have? Are happy left alone to raise your children? Are you happy with having to try to teach your sons how to be men? Are you happy watching your daughters searching for the love they lacked from a father?

It is a natural instinct for women to nest, and seek security. Black women need to stop settling for less. Remember you are the prize to be won. Hold yourself in high esteem and only when a man proves himself worthy should you take on the responsibility of a family. If you continue to settle for less you will continue to do it alone.

When God created Adam and Eve, He gave us the blueprint for the family. In man he instilled certain qualities in support of the family, and He did the same for women. One man and one woman is the correct equation for procreation. The black races in returning to the traditional family need to understand God's intentions. Homosexual marriage and adoption was not part of that plan. Two men or two women are unable to give the well-rounded education needed by children. Many homosexual men claim to feel like women inside, but they are not. They are incapable of giving to a child what a woman is able by nature to give. I know that this may be an unpopular view to espouse, yet I accept the Word of God as the absolute truth. To support homosexuality as right I would have to deny God. I am not going to do that.

The black race's only chance to advance is through the rebuilding of the family. As with many other things that need to be changed the government is powerless to affect the change needed. Only within ourselves can we change our direction and get back on the right track.

LOSE THE GOVERNMENT FIND GOD:

The element in the creation of the United States Government that set it apart and made it the great country it once was, is that its foundations were laid in the Word of God. Without a philosophy   or some higher power defining right from wrong we are left to the morals and judgement of man. What man believes to be right continues to change with who is in power. Reference Germany and Adolph Hitler; under his leadership it was acceptable to exterminate six million Jews. People of different countries throughout history have experienced similar atrocities because their leaders had no spiritual guide. Many in the black race look to our government to supply their daily needs. Our black leaders seek to pass laws that leave us more and more beholden to the government each day. We as a people have transferred the faith that we once held in God and look to the government as our deliverer. Many of us look to the government for our food, our day care and many other parts of our lives that government shouldn't have a role in. Those in power trying to deliver the goodies see their socialist programs as bait to keep the black race marching to the beat of the Liberal's drum. The Liberal politician claims that he/she is the only one who has the best interest of the black race at heart and offers programs that chain the hands of the black race stifling our creativity and keeping many of us on the 21st century plantation.

These socialist policies offered by the liberal party go against everything that the Bible teaches. The Bible teaches us to work for your daily bread, not to sit home waiting for a check on the 1st and 16th of the month. We as a race need to return to the days when we sought the aid of The Almighty and waited for the answer. For as things currently stand we are supporting a political philosophy that despises the God we claim to love so dearly. We need to look to the Word of God to help make the proper choices when giving our support to who will lead this country and where they will lead it. The philosophy of liberalism tells us that we need to separate God from our political decisions. The Black race needs to stop supporting a philosophy that seeks to remove the spiritual guide that keeps us on the right track and protects our freedom. Do we want leaders that make their decisions on the changing winds of time, or do we want leaders guided by the will of God? It is easy to say that all politicians are corrupt and evil, but do we want to support those who openly position themselves against God and choose to lead this country away from the path of righteousness? Can we continue to support a political philosophy that supports late term abortions, homosexual marriage and removing the Ten Commandments from courthouses? Is this really whose hands you wish to be left in?

STEAL THE KNOWLEDGE:

Steal the knowledge speaks of the aggressive attitude that we need to have in the classroom. The inner city schools are in a state of deterioration. School budgets continue to grow as we look for newer and better ways to inspire our children to learn the necessities that will put them on the road to success. While many black children struggle with the basics, what is it that allows some students to excel while others struggle? Our current black leadership would have you believe that the cause is racial. That what is being taught doesn't represent the black experience. We have made excuses and tried to lower the standard so that more students could be successful. What we have accomplished is we've dumbed down of the masses. Instead of setting a high standard and expecting all to reach it, we've dropped the standard in order to make our schools look proficient. Parents no longer can depend on the public schools to educate our children. We must be actively involved ensuring that our children are receiving proper instruction.

I remember my daughter approached me because she was having difficulty understanding how to divide fractions. I told her well dividing fractions is easy, I had just helped her previously on multiplying fraction and explained to her a reciprocal and the procedure. She then showed me the way she was being taught how to divide factions. The procedure she was taught was confusing and inefficient. I became angered that such a simple thing was made difficult. My daughter later told me that her entire class was struggling with the method that was being taught and that she had pulled her friends' aside and showed them the proper procedure. My daughter was approached by the teacher and questioned where she learned to divide fraction like this. My daughter explained to her teacher that her father had instructed her and that I would be more than willing to come in and discuss the teacher's methods. Later my daughter told me that her teacher started teaching the whole class to divide fractions the way I had taught her.

With my daughter I am a lucky father. She seems to understand the importance of an education and she expects to be the best in her class at all things. She has a hunger for knowledge and doesn't give up because the task is difficult. This is the attitude that we in the black race need to have. We need to be confident that we can learn the lessons. So many black children and their parents accept mediocre performance instead of demanding excellence.

BE RIGHT IN ALL YOU DO:

*"Racism is not an excuse
not to do the best we can"*
(Arthur Ashe)

This was what blacks of the past lived by. They never used racism as an excuse to be lazy or worse criminally inclined. Our black elders believed the contrary, they believed that they had to be twice as good and work twice as hard because of racism. Where has that work ethic gone? Because of slavery and the injustice suffered by the black race many today feel justified in their unlawful conduct. Many say "the white man won't give me a chance in the legal world so all I am left with is the underworld." This of course is just a cop out, an excuse for failure and justification for taken the quick and easy road. Doing the right thing is never easy. It usually takes time, commitment, and sacrifice. For years blacks have blamed their failure to prepare for success on the actions of the white community, for it is always easier to blame others than to look in the mirror at the truth. Now I in no way mean to suggest that there haven't been injustice or racism doesn't exist, but like many other blacks who have chosen not to allow these barriers to stop their pursuit for success, I choose to stay the course. The right road to travel is always blocked with obstacles. If it were easy everyone would do it.

Malcolm X taught that blacks needed to cleanse themselves of the "white mans poisons" what he spoke of was the drugs that have decimated our communities, the alcohol that has killed our ambition, and the abuse we have inflicted upon our women. Malcolm X saw these evils as the elements that would lead to our destruction, how right he was.

Today our black youth see no moral problem with selling drugs. The worst part is that they have no conscience about selling it to their own people. Their actions have done more damage to the black race than any anti-black organization including the Ku Klux Klan. Their drugs have killed more children, broken up more homes, enslaved more souls, and destroyed more lives than any racist action.

We stand to lose some of our best and brightest because we have decided on a road of a victim not considering the backlash it would cause inside our communities. So many of us have lost our way absent of real leadership; I once heard a poignant quote *"that in the absence of true leadership you will drink the sand and think its water"*. This is where we find ourselves within the black community. Our leadership attached us to a philosophy void of judgement of right and wrong. What else should we expect than what we have? Should it be any surprise that a group of black teens can get in a car and shoot up a house full of women and children trying to exact revenge on one person? Now I'm sure these were not the intentions of our leaders, but they chose a direction where God wasn't present, where right isn't always right and there's always an excuse for doing wrong.

If we hope to survive within our communities we must do what we know to be right. We must stop making excuses for the shortcomings we have, and to accept the Word of God as our reference. We must stop using past injustice, as an excuse for our failures, instead let's show our children real character and continue to try. Let's stop telling our children why they can't succeed and let's by example show them that they can. Let's exorcise the evils that Malcolm X warned us of, and let us put or faith in God to lead us to a better day.

WALK WITH HONOR AND DIGNITY:

The black race has suffered great injustice and persecution. Yet, through it all have kept their dignity. Dr. Martin Luther King Jr. asked the difficult task of non-violent protest from his followers. How many of us today could show such self-control. In the face of violence and brutality show restraint and not retaliate. Dr. King looked to a higher power something bigger than us all, and in this we were able to hold our heads high and demand the respect and rights that had for so long been denied us.

The black race has much to be proud of; we have had great inventors, scholars, doctors, lawyers, and artist. We have made contributions of unmeasureable value to this country and the world. Our children need to know the accomplishments of our people and that we hold a stake in the future of this country and the direction it will follow. But, like in all races we have those among us who seek only destruction and to profit from others hardships. The drug dealers, the thieves, and the cowards that walk away from their children are the ones who we must disassociate with and stop claiming as our identifiers.

I was listening to a comic recently, and he spoke of how much black people missed President Bill Clinton and how we associated with him because of his indiscretions. The funniest humor is always the description of real life. Many of us in the black community have a low opinion of what black is. I have always looked to people like Dr. King, W.E. B. Dubois, Dr. Rice, Congressman Watts, and my father James H. Brown Sr. to define what black is. I have always looked to those who walk with honor and dignity for my guidance and my strength.

We decided to write this book because we have seen the effects that living life by a liberal philosophy has had on the black community. In order to make a change we must be willing to take an honest look at ourselves and be willing to confront our problems. Many who have looked at early versions of this work have stated that the problems that we speak of are not only in the black community and I agree. I explain that if on my way home I see my entire block on fire, where am I going to go first. Of coarse I am going to take care of home first.

I truly believe that we can fix the problems within the black community. We are a talented and resourceful people. Look at all that we have accomplished through the years with the challenges that we've faced. I believe that we must have a national recognition that we are on the wrong course, and those in poverty are adversely affected the most.

I recently watched an episode of The Larry Elders Show. This particular episode was an update on earlier guest. Larry had two young black children that were out of control, trouble in school, selling drugs, and premature dating many of the problems that we have in our communities. Through Larry Elder's intervention these children were able to get on the right course, to see the error of their ways. It touched my heart to see that a difference was possible. Now all stories won't have a happy ending and there will always be causalities, but if enough of us believe that we can make it better, than I believe we can. I pray that this work touches those who read it and it is understood that it was written with love and hope for a better day.

THE END

BIBLIOGRAPHY

A Brief History of Hobson City, Alabama. The Peoples Journal: 27 July 1899 p2 col.4

Barton, David. The Myth of Separation Texas: WallBuilder Press. 1992

Boller, F. Paul Jr. Presidential Campaigns: Oxford University Press, 1984 1985

Brown, James Sr. Personal Interview 21 May 2004

Cramer, Clayton E., The Racist Roots of Gun Control: Copyright 1993
July 27, 2004 http:// www.firearmsandliberty.com/cramer.racism.html

Davis, Ronald PH.D, Surviving Jim Crow, The History of Jim Crow 17 May 2004
<http://www.jimcrowhistroy.org/history/surviving.htm

D"Souza Dinesh, The End of Racism Free Press Paperbacks
New York, New York 1995.

Encyclopedia Britannica 2004 Ultimate Reference Suite CD
Copyright 2004. Encyclopedia Britannica Inc.

Fletcher A. Michael and Kevin Merida, Jurist Embraces Image as a Hard-Line Holdout
Washington Post October 11, 2004; Page A01, 4/23/05
http://www.washingtonpost.com/ac2/wp-dyn/A22735-2004Oct10?language=printer

Franklin, John Hope. From Slavery To Freedom A History of Negro Americans.3rd ed.
New York: Vintage Books 1947.

Kincaid, Cliff Al Sharpton And Moral Values, Media Monitor January 5, 2005
http://www.aim.org/media_monitor_print/2399_0_2_0, 5/13/05 3:56 PM

King, Dr. Martin Luther Jr., I Have a Dream, Speech, August 28 1963, Washington D.C.

National Security Counsel, Biography of Condoleeza rice, National security Advisor, 4/21/05
http:// www.whitehouse.gov/nsc/ricebio.html

Nordlinger, Jay Power Dem National Review Feature Article Jay Nordlinger On The Rise To
Power Of Al Sharpton, March 20, 2000.
http://www.nationalreview.com/20Mar00/nordlinger03200.html

Madamaga, Anwar Dr. Personal Interview 21 May 2004

Perryman, Wayne Unfounded Loyalty 2nd edition
Hara Publishing Seattle, Washington 2004

Schaffer, Richard T, Sociology A Brief Introduction 5th ed.
New York: McGraw Hill Companies Inc. 2004

Timmerman, Kenneth R. Shakedown
Regnery Publishing, Inc,2002 Washington D.C
Williams, Armstrong NAACP Head Mfume Didn't Retire, He Was Booted Out Dec 6, 2004
http://www.humaneventsonline.com/article.php?print=yes&id=5954

www.ingramcontent.com/pod-product-compliance
Lightning Source LLC
Chambersburg PA
CBHW031514270326
41930CB00006B/401